BELLEVUE PALACE
Bern

PAGES BLANCHES

**Das Hotel Bellevue
Palace in Bern**

**The Bellevue Palace
Hotel in Berne**

Der Autor / The Author

Martin Fröhlich (*1940), Dr. sc. techn., ist Architekt, Architekturhistoriker und Mitglied des Wissenschaftlichen Beirats des Nachdiplomstudiums Denkmalpflege und Umnutzung der Berner Fachhochschule in Burgdorf.

Martin Fröhlich (b. 1940), Dr. sc. techn., is an architect, architectural historian and a senior tutor for post-graduate studies in Conservation and Reallocation of Historical Monuments at the University of Applied Sciences in Burgdorf.

Martin Fröhlich. Das Hotel Bellevue Palace in Bern.
Das Werk basiert auf dem Text des Schweizerischen Kunstführers
Das Hotel Bellevue Palace in Bern von Martin Fröhlich, Bern 2006.
Der Text wurde für diese Publikation bearbeitet und ergänzt durch Thomas Bolt.

Martin Fröhlich. The Bellevue Palace Hotel in Berne, Switzerland.
The book is based on the text in the Guides to Swiss Monuments *The Bellevue Palace Hotel in Berne,* by Martin Fröhlich, Berne 2006 revised and complemented by Thomas Bolt for the current edition.

Herausgeber / Published by
Gesellschaft für Schweizerische Kunstgeschichte GSK, Bern
Das Hotel Bellevue Palace in Bern
Diese Publikation erscheint in der Reihe «Pages blanches» der Gesellschaft für Schweizerische Kunstgeschichte GSK, Bern.
Vertrieb: GSK, Bern
Society for the History of Swiss Art SHSA, Berne
The Bellevue Palace Hotel in Berne
This publication is part of the «Pages blanches» series of the Society for the History of Swiss Art SHSA, Berne.
Distributed by SHSA, Berne, Switzerland.

GSK Projektleitung – SHAS Project management: Nicole Bauermeister
Redaktion (dt.) – German editor: Thomas Bolt, GSK/SHSA
Redaktion (engl.) – English editor: GSK/SHSA
Übersetzung ins Englische (2006) – Translation into English (2006):
Jenny Haller-Pratt, Bern – *Teilübersetzung und Lektorat Englisch dieser Ausgabe (2013) – Partial translation into and editing of the 2013 English version:*
Margret Powell-Joss, Oban, Scotland, UK

Konzept und Gestaltung – Concept and design: Philipp Kirchner, GSK/SHSA
Bildbearbeitung – Image editing and processing: Philipp Kirchner, GSK/SHSA
Druckvorstufe und Druck – Pre-press and printing: Imprimerie Gasser SA, Le Locle
Einband – Binding: Buchbinderei Burkhardt AG, Mönchaltorf

ISSN: 2235-3461
ISBN: 978-3-03797-082-9

© 2013 Gesellschaft für Schweizerische Kunstgeschichte GSK, Bern, Schweiz – Society for the History of Swiss Art SHSA, Berne, Switzerland. All rights reserved Dieses Werk ist urheberrechtlich geschützt. Die dadurch begründeten Rechte, insbesondere die der Übersetzung, des Nachdrucks, des Vortrags, der Entnahme von Abbildungen und Tabellen, der Funksendung, der Mikroverfilmung oder der Vervielfältigung auf anderen Wegen und der Speicherung in Datenverarbeitungsanlagen, bleiben, auch bei nur auszugsweiser Verwertung, vorbehalten. Eine Vervielfältigung dieses Werks oder von Teilen dieses Werks ist auch im Einzelfall nur in den Grenzen der Bestimmungen des Urheberrechtsgesetzes in der jeweils geltenden Fassung zulässig. Sie ist grundsätzlich vergütungspflichtig. Zuwiderhandlungen unterliegen den Strafbestimmungen des Urheberrechts. –
This book contains material protected under International and Swiss Copyright Laws and Treaties. Any unauthorised reprint, translation or use of this material is prohibited. No part of this book may be reproduced or transmitted in any form or by any means, electronic or mechanical, including photocopying, recording, or by any information storage and retrieval system without prior written permission from the publisher. Equitable remuneration will be required to be paid to the publisher for reproductions of any kind. Any unauthorised use of material contained in this book will be prosecuted to the maximum extent possible under law.

Inhalt

Vorwort der Gesellschaft für Schweizerische Kunstgeschichte	6
Vorwort von Bundesrätin Eveline Widmer-Schlumpf	8

Das Hotel Bellevue Palace in Bern — 11

Einleitung — 13
   Das Stadthotel par excellence — 13
   Bern um 1900 — 16
   La belle vie – la belle vue. Warum das Hotel Bellevue «Bellevue» heisst — 22

Der Vorgängerbau. Das Hotel Bellevue von 1864–1865 — 27
   Ein Blick in die Geschichte — 27
   Die Familie Osswald — 30

Der Bau des Hotels Bellevue Palace 1911–1913 — 37
   Die Gunst der Stunde genutzt — 37
   Stahlbetonskelett und Klimaanlage – In Rekordzeit gebaut und technisch auf dem neusten Stand — 39
   Die Architekten — 43
   Das «Adlon von Bern» – Ein Stück Berner «Schokoladeseite» — 44
   Vom Generalsquartier zum Bundeshotel — 51

Vom Glanz des Bellevue Palace – Ein Spaziergang durch die Räumlichkeiten — 71
   Eingangshalle und Palmengarten — 71
   Salon d'Honneur und La Terrasse — 71
   Salon Casino (kleiner Speisesaal) und Salon Rouge — 80
   Salon du Palais (Speisesaal) — 86
   Salon Royal (ehemalige Hotelhalle) — 86
   Bar, ehemaliges Billardzimmer, Restaurant Zur Münz und Grillroom — 90
   Konferenzgeschoss — 93
   Gästezimmer — 94

Die Gästebücher — 98
   Die Gäste — 100

Anmerkungen — 106
Quellen/Bibliografie — 107
Bildnachweis — 107

Table of Contents

Foreword by the Society for the History of Swiss Art	6
Foreword by Eveline Widmer-Schlumpf, Federal Councillor	8

The Bellevue Palace Hotel in Berne — 11

Introduction — 13
   A city hotel — 13
   Berne, ca. 1900 — 16
   La belle vie – la belle vue. How the Bellevue Hotel came by its name — 22

The Predecessor Building, or the old Bellevue Hotel — 27
   A glance at history — 27
   The Osswald family — 30

Construction of the Bellevue Palace Hotel — 37
   Seizing the moment — 37
   The new building with its concrete skeleton and air-conditioning – state-of-the-art and built in record time — 39
   The architecs — 43
   The «Adlon of Berne» – seeing Berne at its best — 44
   From the General's headquarters to government guest-house — 51

A Tour of the Glorious Bellevue Palace — 71
   The Hotel lobby and the Palm Garden — 71
   The dining-rooms: Salon d'Honneur and La Terrasse — 71
   Salon Casino (small dining-room) and Salon Rouge — 80
   Salon du Palais (dining-room) — 86
   Salon Royal (former hotel lobby) — 86
   Bar, former Billiards Room, Restaurant Zur Münz and Grill Room — 90
   The conference floor — 93
   The guest rooms and suites — 94

The Visitor's Books — 98
   The guests — 100

Notes — 106
Credits/Bibliography — 107
Photo Credits — 107

Vorwort der Gesellschaft für Schweizerische Kunstgeschichte
Foreword by the Society for the History of Swiss Art

Als klassisches Tourismusland besitzt die Schweiz einen grossen Reichtum an vielgestaltiger Hotelarchitektur der gehobenen und luxuriösen Klasse. Stadthotels an Seen und Flüssen, Hotels in stadtnaher oder freier Aussichtslage, Hotels in hochalpinen Sport- und Feriendestinationen, Kur- und Bäderhotels mit langer Tradition – in allen Regionen unseres viersprachigen Landes setzte die Hotellerie spätestens seit dem frühen 19. Jahrhundert internationale Massstäbe.

Etwas hat das nun hundertjährige Bellevue Palace in Bern allen anderen Hotels der Schweiz voraus: Es steht quasi im Dienst der Schweizerischen Eidgenossenschaft und deren Repräsentationen und Gäste. Während der Sessionen der Eidgenössischen Räte ist das «Bellevue» bisweilen gar inoffizieller Schauplatz des hektischen Politbetriebs. Diese Rollen spiegeln sich in seiner Lage in Berns Altstadt, am Anfang der langen Bauflucht mit den beiden flankierenden Bundeshäusern und dem zentralen Parlamentsgebäude, diesen so unhelvetisch auftrumpfenden Historismus-Architekturen des jungen Bundesstaates. Während die Staatsgebäude den Renaissancestil der italienischen Signorien und Rathäuser nachempfinden, ist das Hotel Bellevue Palace dem

As a classic tourist destination Switzerland boasts a great diversity in and wealth of first-class and luxurious hotel architecture. City hotels on lakeshores and river banks, hotels in a leafy suburban setting or with stunning views, resort hotels in the Alps, historic spa hotels – since the early 19th century at least, the hotel industry has been setting international benchmarks in every region of our quadrilingual country.

The Bellevue Palace Hotel in Berne, which opened its doors one-hundred years ago, is ahead of any other hotels in Switzerland, however, insofar as it is the venue of Swiss government receptions and the abode of Switzerland's official guests. The hotel can be said to be in the service of the Swiss Confederation. During the sessions of the Swiss parliament, moreover, the Bellevue quite frequently provides the inofficial venue for hectic political discussions and negotiations. These roles are reflected in its situation in the Old City of Berne, where the hotel constitutes a cornerstone in the line of architectural structures that includes the two administrative wings flanking the Federal Palace. In the government buildings the fledgling confederation very un-Helvetically asserted itself in a historicist style that emulates the seigno-

klassizistischen Baustil der Schlösser und Paläste der europäischen Monarchien im 18. und 19. Jahrhundert verpflichtet. Mondän-elegant wenn auch nicht dekorativ überladen sollte dieses Hotel vis-à-vis des schönsten Alpenpanoramas seine internationalen Touristen und Staatsgäste empfangen. Und sowieso hatte es komfortabel zu sein, musste es über die modernsten technischen und sanitären Einrichtungen verfügen!

Nach einem ereignisreichen Jahrhundert hochstehender Gastlichkeit feiert nun also das Bellevue Palace sein rundes Jubiläum. Dass es dieses auf so stilvolle Art mit einer Publikation in unserer noch jungen Buchreihe Pages blanches tut, erfüllt die Gesellschaft für Schweizerische Kunstgeschichte in Bern mit Freude und auch mit etwas Stolz. Wir danken Herrn Urs Bührer, dem Direktor des Bellevue Palace, für seine wertvolle Unterstützung. Ein besonderer Dank gilt dem Buchautor Dr. Martin Fröhlich, dem exzellenten Kenner dieses Kulturdenkmals. Als Projektleiterin sei Nicole Bauermeister, Direktorin der GSK, dankend erwähnt ebenso wie Thomas Bolt und Philippe Kirchner von der GSK für Redaktion und Gestaltung, und die Übersetzerinnen der englischen Version, Jenny Haller-Pratt und Margret Powell-Joss.

Dem Hotel Bellevue Palace wünscht die GSK weiterhin viel Erfolg bei ihrem Dienst an der Gastfreundschaft!

Benno Schubiger, Präsident der Gesellschaft für Schweizerische Kunstgeschichte GSK

ries and townhalls of the Italian Renaissance. The style of the Bellevue Palace Hotel, on the other hand, has been inspired by Europe's classicist 18th and 19th-century castles and palaces. Facing the spectacular panorama of the Alps, the hotel was designed to receive international tourists and state visitors alike in an elegant and sophisticated, but nevertheless understated setting. And, of course, it had to be at the cutting edge of technology and sanitation to provide every conceivable comfort!

Now the Bellevue Palace Hotel can look back across an eventful century of hospitality of the highest standard. That it should celebrate its centenary in the form of a stylish publication in our recently-launched Pages blanches series is cause for rejoicing to the Society for the History of Swiss Art SHSA in Berne, and for a little pride. We are indebted to Urs Bührer, the Director of the Bellevue Palace Hotel, for his valuable support. Our special thanks go to the author of this book, Dr. Martin Fröhlich, who knows this cultural monument inside and out. We would also like to mention project manager, Nicole Bauermeister, SHSA Director, as well as SHSA editor Thomas Bolt, SHSA designer Philippe Kirchner, and the translators of the English version, Jenny Haller-Pratt and Margret Powell-Joss.

The SHSA wishes the Bellevue Palace Hotel much success in its continued services to first-class hospitality.

Benno Schubiger, President, Society for the History of Swiss Art SHSA

Vorwort von Bundesrätin Eveline Widmer-Schlumpf
Foreword by Eveline Widmer-Schlumpf, Federal Councillor

100 Jahre Bellevue Palace

2013 feiert das «neue» Bellevue Palace in Bern seinen einhundertsten Geburtstag. Das klassische Grandhotel ist als Gästehaus der Schweizer Eidgenossenschaft von historischer, kultureller und nationaler Bedeutung. Die Geschichte des im Stil der neoklassizistischen Reformarchitektur erbauten Fünfsternehauses ist ereignisvoll und legendär.

Als Bern im Jahr 1848 zur Bundesstadt der Schweiz gewählt wurde, setzte mit den damit verbundenen Auflagen, den eidgenössischen Räten und der Bundesverwaltung die notwendigen Infrastrukturen und Räumlichkeiten zur Verfügung zu stellen, ein wahrer Bauboom ein. Dazu gehörte der Bau eines repräsentativen Hotels in der Nähe des Bundeshauses. Am 27. November 1913 öffnete das Bellevue Palace seine Türen. Es war fortan Inbegriff moderner Grand Hotellerie, für Raum und Komfort. Heute gehört es, als Ensemble mit dem Bundeshaus, sicherlich zu den eindrücklichsten Bauwerken seiner Art in der Schweiz.

Das Hotel Bellevue Palace wurde 1976 von der Schweizerischen Nationalbank übernommen. Seit 1994 befindet es sich im Besitz der Schweizerischen Eidgenossenschaft.

The Bellevue Palace Hotel – celebrating 100 years

In 2013 the «new» Bellevue Palace Hotel in Berne can celebrate its 100th anniversary. The classic grand-hotel is the Swiss Confederation's «guest house» and of historic, cultural and national significance. The five-star establishment built in the neo-classicist style of reform architecture evoks an eventful and legendary history.

The decision in 1848 for Berne to be the Swiss Confederation's capital city triggered a veritable construction boom as requirements had to be met to provide accommodation and infrastructure to the Federal government, Parliament and Administration. A prestigious hotel in close proximity of the Federal Palace also needed to be built. The new Bellevue Palace Hotel opened its doors on 27th November, 1913, immediately setting a benchmark in terms of the space and comfort expected of modern grand-hotels. Today the hotel, in conjunction with the Federal Palace, constitutes one of Switzerland's most iconic architectural ensembles.

In 1976 ownership of the Bellevue Palace Hotel was transferred the Swiss National Bank; it has been the property of the Swiss Confederation since 1994.

Schon das «alte» Bellevue spielte seit 1865 eine zentrale Rolle bei offiziellen Anlässen der Landesregierung. Heute empfängt, beherbergt und betreut das Fünfsternehaus in würdigem Rahmen und mit gelebter Schweizer Gastfreundschaft unsere Staatsgäste und die Delegationen der Eidgenossenschaft. Auch für das diplomatische Corps ist es ein wichtiger Bestandteil der Hauptstadt und während der Sessionen des Eidgenössischen Parlamentes ist das Haus ein Drehpunkt des politischen Lebens.

Das Bellevue Palace ist in den vergangenen 100 Jahren zu einer festen Institution geworden. Ich wünsche «unserem Gästehaus» weiterhin viel Erfolg.

Eveline Widmer-Schlumpf
Bundesrätin

Since 1865 already, the «old» Bellevue Hotel played a key role as a venue of official events hosted by the Swiss Federal Government. Today's five-star establishment embodies warm Swiss hospitality. Switzerland's state visitors and federal delegations are made welcome and looked after in a privileged setting. The diplomatic corps consider the hotel an important element of the Swiss capital and during Swiss parliamentary sessions, the hotel is a vibrant hub in the country's political life.

In the course of the past century the Bellevue Palace Hotel has been an enduring institution. May «our guest house» continue to enjoy great succes!

Eveline Widmer-Schlumpf
Federal Councillor

**Das Hotel Bellevue
Palace in Bern**

Martin Fröhlich

**The Bellevue Palace
Hotel in Berne**

Einleitung
Introduction

Das Stadthotel par excellence

Das «Bellevue», wie das noble Fünfsternehotel Bellevue Palace an der Kochergasse in Bern liebevoll genannt wird, gehört ebenso zur Identität der Schweizer Bundesstadt wie etwa das Parlamentsgebäude, das Münster, der Zytgloggeturm oder der Bärengraben. Das «Bellevue» verkörpert Berner Gastlichkeit und Gastfreundschaft in höchster Vollendung und verbindet gepflegte Distanziertheit mit einnehmender Herzlichkeit und Weltoffenheit.

Seine Geschichte reicht zurück in die Mitte der 40er-Jahre des 19. Jahrhunderts zum berühmten Berner Gasthof «Goldener Falken», wo für die Gäste wohl alles noch etwas einfacher zu und her ging und die Zimmerschlüssel vermutlich hinter dem Ausschanktresen in der Gaststube aufgehängt waren. Weitergeführt wurde der Betrieb ab 1865 vom damaligen «Falken»-Wirt im neu errichteten «Bellevue» an der Inselgasse (heute Kochergasse), nun per definitionem als «richtiges» Hotel, wo der Concierge die Gäste an der separierten Réception begrüsste und speziell geschultes Personal die Bedürfnisse und Wünsche der Gäste zu erfüllen wusste.[1] Schliesslich entstand zwischen 1911 und 1913 der imposante Belle-Époque-Bau des Grandhotels mit grosszügiger di-

A city hotel

The locals have lovingly shortened the name of the Bellevue Palace Hotel at no. 2 Kochergasse in Berne to «the Bellevue». The elegant five-star establishment has made its mark on the identity of the Swiss capital city as much as the city's *Bundeshaus* [Federal Palace], *Münster* [Cathedral], *Zytglogge* [Clock Tower] or *Bärengraben* [Bear Pit].

The epitome of Bernese hospitality, the Bellevue Palace combines distinguished sophistication with engaging warmth and cosmopolitanism. Its history begins in the mid-1840s, with a then-famous yet fairly modest Bernese inn called the Goldener Falken in Münstergasse, where a rack of hooks behind the counter in the tavern would have held the room keys. In 1865 the Falken landlord relocated his business to the newly completed «Bellevue» hotel in Kochergasse, a «proper» hotel whose concierge welcomed arrivals at a dedicated reception desk and specially trained staff fulfilled their guests' needs and special requests.[1]

Eventually, superceding its smaller predecessor, the Bellevue, an imposing grand-hotel in the style of the *Belle époque* was built on the same spot from 1911–1913 to provide more spacious reception halls and parlours on the ground floor,

1 Bellevue Palace u. Grandhotel Bernerhof Bern. Plakat von Emil Cardinaux, 1934. – Poster designed by Emil Cardinaux, 1934.

2 «Kirchenfeldbrücke mit Bundespalast und Palace Hotel Bellevue». Postkarte 1939. – Kirchenfeld bridge with Federal Parliament Buildings and Bellevue Palace Hotel. Postcard, 1939.

mensionierten Repräsentationsräumlichkeiten und Salons im Erdgeschoss und einer Beletage (im 3. Stockwerk) mit den vornehmen Suiten und Zimmern. Das luxuriös eingerichtete Gästehaus wurde anstelle des kleineren Vorgängerhotels «Bellevue» von Grund auf neu erbaut und eröffnete als Grandhotel Bellevue Palace am 27. November 1913 mit einem glanzvollen Festanlass mit 2000 Geladenen.

Das «Bellevue Palace» verkörpert damit in exemplarischer Weise den Typus des Stadthotels. Innerhalb der Entwicklungsgeschichte nimmt es dennoch eine privilegierte Stellung ein: Seine zentrumsnahe, verkehrstechnisch bestens erschlossene Lage und die einzigartige Aussicht in die Berner Alpenkette mit Eiger, Mönch und Jungfrau machen das «Bellevue Palace» zum Stadthotel par excellence.

Gästelisten und Gästebücher berichten von ungezählten Besucherinnen und Besuchern, von bedeutenden und illustren Persönlichkeiten aus Kultur, Politik, Wirtschaft und Showbusiness, die in den vergangenen einhundert Jahren in Kutschen, hochglanzpolierten Luxuslimusinen und Staatskarossen beim Hoteleingang vorfuhren und im Hotel Bellevue Palace logierten. Im Ersten Weltkrieg diente es als Generalhauptquartier der Schweizer Armee und wurde insbesondere während des Zweiten Weltkriegs sowohl für die internationale Diplomatie als auch für die verschwiegenen Geheimdienste zur idealen «Informationsdrehscheibe» auf neutralem Boden. Das weltweit geschätzte Grandhotel nutzte den Vorteil seiner unmittelbaren Nachbarschaft zum Bundeshaus, dem politischen Zentrum der Schweiz, und etablierte sich auch als Staatshotel und heimliche «Dépendance der Macht».

and a *piano nobile* with very elegant rooms and suites (on the third floor). The brand-new luxury establishment was inaugurated on 27th November 1913, when two thousand invited guests attended the glamorous festivities at the Bellevue Palace Grand-Hotel.

Since then the Bellevue Palace has been the epitome of a city hotel. Moreover, it occupies a privileged position in Berne's urban fabric due to its central location, with excellent access to every form of transport, and its unique views of the Bernese Alps with the Eiger, Mönch and Jungfrau peaks.

Guest lists and visitors' books name a great many illustrious guests from the realms of business, culture, politics and show business who came to stay at the Bellevue Palace Hotel, arriving in horse-drawn coaches, state landaus and gleaming limousines. During the First World War, the hotel was the general headquarters of the Swiss Army, an ideal information hub on neutral territory, both for international diplomats and taciturn secret service agents. Enjoying an excellent reputation all over the world, and making the most of its immediate vicinity to the Federal Palace, the hub of Swiss politics, the Bellevue Palace also established itself as the «state» hotel and secret «annexe of power».

However, the Bellevue Palace is rather more than just a grand hotel and the Swiss Government's guest house. In urbanistic terms it also forms an important part of the southern aspect of Berne's Old City. Together with the Casino, which belongs to the Burgergemeinde [Association of Burghers], it represents the southern gateway to Berne at the top of Kirchenfeldbrücke, the bridge across the Aare river, which opened in 1881. Berne's best side can be seen

3 Der Bärenplatz um 1905. Im Hintergrund das 1902 eingeweihte Parlamentsgebäude. – Bärenplatz in Berne's city centre, ca. 1905; in the background the Federal Parliament Building inaugurated in 1902.

4 Stadtansicht von Südosten. Links die Bundesbauten, das Hotel Bellevue und das Casino, rechts anschliessend die Bauten der Berner Altstadt. Postkarte um 1925. – View of the city of Berne from the south-east. Left: Federal Palace, the Bellevue Hotel and the Casino; further right, the houses of the Old City of Berne. Postcard, ca. 1925.

Das «Bellevue Palace» ist jedoch nicht nur ein Luxushotel und nicht nur das Gästehaus der Eidgenossenschaft, es ist auch als Bauwerk ein wichtiges städtebauliches Element in der Südfront der Altstadt von Bern. Zusammen mit dem ihm gegenüberliegenden Casino der Berner Burgergemeinde bildet es das südliche «Stadttor» an der 1881 eröffneten Kirchenfeldbrücke. Diese Stadtansicht zeigt Berns «Schokoladenseite». Hier reihen sich – als Rahmen der Altstadt – die stattlichen Repräsentationsbauten des späten 19. und frühen 20. Jahrhunderts: Der Bernerhof, 1856–1858 erbaut von Jakob Friedrich Studer und Johann Carl Dähler, das ehemalige Bundes-Rathaus, heute Bundeshaus West, 1852–1857 ebenfalls von Studer, das Parlamentsgebäude, 1894–1902, und das Bundeshaus Ost, 1888–1892, beide von Hans Wilhelm Auer. Den östlichen Abschluss dieser beeindruckenden «Architekturfassade» bilden das 1911–1913 von Paul Lindt und Max Hofmann errichtete Hotel Bellevue Palace und – auf der anderen Seite des Brückenkopfs der Kirchenfeldbrücke – das Casino, 1906–1908, ebenfalls von Lindt und Hofmann. Erst anschliessend wird die mittelalterliche und neuzeitliche Bebauung der Stadt sichtbar. An dieser Schlüsselstelle fungiert das Hotel Bellevue Palace als wichtiger «Pfeiler» des Stadtzugangs und «reagiert» mit seiner Architektur sowohl auf den Blick von der Kirchenfeldbrücke her als auch auf die Aussicht in die Berner Alpen.

Bern um 1900

Das Hotel Bellevue Palace entstand in der Zeit zwischen der Jahrhundertwende zum 20. Jahrhundert und dem Ersten Weltkrieg. Diese Jahre verstanden sich als Reformzeit:

from the bridge. From here, the visitor can admire the row of prestigious buildings dating back to the late 19th and early 20th centuries that provide a frame to the Old City, i.e. the Bernerhof, built in 1856–1858 by Jakob Friedrich Studer and Johann Carl Dähler; the East Wing of the Federal Palace, built by Hans Wilhelm Auer in 1888–1892; the Parliament building proper, 1894–1902, also by Auer; and the former Federal State House, today's West Wing of the Federal Palace, 1852–1857, again by Studer. These were followed by the Bellevue Palace Hotel, built in 1911–1913 by Paul Lindt and Max Hofmann and – on the opposite side of the top of Kirchenfeld Bridge – the *Burgergemeinde*-owned Casino, built in 1906–1908, also by Lindt and Hofmann. These additions highlight the city's Medieval and modern developments alike. In this key location the Bellevue Palace Hotel functions as an important «pillar» in the structure of gateways to the city. In its architecture, the building responds both to the view of the Alps and to the view from Kirchenfeld Bridge.

Berne, ca. 1900

The Bellevue Palace was built in the era which lasted from the turn of the 19th/20th centuries until the First World War and would come to be derided as Late Historicism. Those years, however, saw numerous reforms, with crinolines being consigned to the dustbin, for example, making way for lighter and more loosely fitted ladies' wear.

A spirit of optimism entered Berne in the early 1890s: from 1891 the new hydro-electricity plant in Bern's low-lying Matte quarter supplied power for the city's electrical

Die Reifröcke wanderten auf den Müll und machten leichten anschmiegsamen Damenkleidern Platz. In Bern herrschte seit etwa 1890 wieder umtriebige Aufbruchstimmung. Ab 1891 lieferte das Elektrizitätswerk an der Aare im Mattequartier Strom für die elektrische Beleuchtung, und das erste Wasserleitungsnetz der Stadt ermöglichte u. a. schon im alten Hotel Bellevue fliessendes Wasser in den Zimmern. Die Hauptstadt erlebte einen eigentlichen Wirtschafts- und Tourismusboom und glich damals einem riesigen Bauplatz.

In dieser Zeit des Aufbruchs und der Erneuerung entstanden einige für die damalige Architekturauffassung typische, das Berner Stadtbild prägende Bauten. Dazu gehören neben Privat- und Geschäftshäusern auch Repräsentationsbauten: das Bernische Historische Museum 1892–1894, auf der grossen Schanze oberhalb der Bahnlinie 1906–1910 das Berner Obergericht und 1903 die Universität, 1908–1912 die Schweizerische Nationalbank am Bundesplatz 1 und – wie erwähnt – das Casino sowie das Hotel Bellevue Palace.

Die zu neuem Leben erwachte Investitionslust der Berner Aristokratie und der Pioniergeist des bernischen Unternehmertums förderte die wirtschaftliche Prosperität im gesamten Kanton. Die modernen Errungenschaften Elektrizität und Stromproduktion machten Vieles möglich. Die Inbetriebnahme der Montreux-Oberland-Bahn und die Realisierung der Löschbergbahnlinie brachten die optimale Anbindung des Berner Oberlandes an das internationale Bahnverkehrsnetz. 1913 führte die stärkste, elektrisch betriebene Lokomotive der Welt erstmals eine Zugskomposition über die Lötschberg-Bergstrecke von Spiez nach Brig.[2] Interlaken und Gstaad entwickelten sich rasch zu den meist

lighting, and the first municipal mains water grid provided establishments and households with running water, including the rooms at the Bellevue Hotel. Much of Berne looked like a gigantic construction site as Switzerland's capital experienced a veritable economic and tourist boom.

At a time which regarded itself as an era of awakening and gentle renewal but was later disparaged as an era of decline, Berne City Council acquired several buildings that have only recently received a more positive appraisal, among them a number of prestigious buildings such as Berne's Historical Museum, 1892–1894 by Lambert and Stahl; the Supreme Court building on Grosse Schanze, 1906–1910 by Bracher, Widmer and Daxelhofer; the Swiss National Bank on Bundesplatz, 1908–1912 by Eduard Joos; and – as mentioned above – the Casino and the Bellevue Palace Hotel, both built by Lindt and Hofmann architects – as well as private and business premises built by Eduard Joos, Karl Indermühle and others.

The Bernese artistocracy's re-kindled desire to invest, and the pioneering spirit of Berne's entrepreneurs powered economic prosperity across the entire canton. The modern commodity of electricity and its more prolific production brought about many changes, among them the inauguration of the Montreux-Oberland railway (MOB) and the completion of the Lötschberg railway line (BLS) in 1913. From the day the most powerful electrical locomotive of its day pulled the first carriages along the Lötschberg mountain route from Spiez to Brig,[2] the canton of Berne was fully connected to the international railway network, which swiftly transformed the small and sleepy villages of Interlaken

besuchten Zentren des mondänen Alpentourismus im Berner Oberland. Mit der Eröffnung zahlreicher Luxushotels und dem erfolgreichen Bau einer Zahnradbahn auf das Jungfraujoch 1912 hatte sich die unwirtliche Bergwelt mit einem Schlag zur bequem erreichbaren grandiosen Erholungskulisse gewandelt. Selbst auf der Kleinen Scheidegg auf über 2000 Metern ü. M. errichtete man unmittelbar unterhalb von Eiger, Mönch und Jungfrau eine Luxusherberge, die den anspruchsvollen Gästen sämtliche Annehmlichkeiten der damaligen Zeit bieten konnte. Und auch sie trug den Namen «Bellevue». «Bellevue» wurde zum Synonym für grossbürgerlichen Lebensgenuss und stand gleichzeitig für die Sehnsucht nach dem Besonderen, dem Unverbrauchten, dem Ultimativen. Ein einzigartiger Kristallisations- und zugleich Kulminationspunkt der Belle Époque war die Jungfernfahrt und der Untergang der «RMS Titanic», des zur damaligen Zeit grössten Luxusdampfers der Welt, im April 1912. Der neue Geist der «Belle Époque» zwischen etwa 1880 und dem Ersten Weltkrieg, zeigte sich auf den Boulevards der Metropolen, in den Cafés und Cabarets, den Ateliers und Galerien, den Konzertsälen und Salons. Architektur, Bildende Kunst und gesellschaftlicher Lebensstil entwickelten sich besonders vielgestaltig und kraftvoll. Das neue Lebensgefühl brachte auch frischen Wind in die Gassen und Lauben von Bern. Die Trambahn fuhr mitten durch die «Einkaufsmeile» der Altstadt vom Bärengraben über den Bahnhof bis hinauf zum Bremgartenfriedhof. Vornehme Touristen aber auch Damen und Herren der einheimischen aristokratischen Oberschicht flanierten über die neuen Boulevards, in den Parkanlagen und in den neu

and Gstaad into the most popular tourist resorts in the Bernese Alps.

The creation of numerous luxury hotels and the successful completion of a rack-and-pinion railway to the Jungfraujoch in 1912 suddenly transformed the once forbidding mountains into a stunning and easily accessible arena of recreation. A luxury inn was built at the great height of 2000 metres above sea level (over 6,500 ft), on the plateau of Kleine Scheidegg. Overlooked by the Eiger, Mönch and Jungfrau peaks, the new hotel – also named «Bellevue» – would provide discerning guests with any convenience conceivable at the time. Epitomising a yearning for something pristine and untainted, special and unique special, for unparalleled novelty, *Bellevue* was synonymous with grand-bourgeois indulgence. One of the *Belle Epoque's* most poignant crystallisation and culmination points was the sinking in April 1912 of RMS Titanic, then the world's biggest luxury liner.

The *Belle Epoque* from about 1880 until the First World War expressed itself in Europe's urban boulevards, cafés and cabarets, art studios and galleries, salons and concert halls. The many changes affected architecture, the fine arts and lifestyles. Nor did Berne's narrow streets and *Lauben* [arcades] remain untouched by this breath of fresh air. Tramways carried passengers through the heart of the Old City, along the «shopping mile» between Bärengraben and the railway station, and on to the cemetery called Bremgartenfriedhof. The ladies and gentlemen of the local aristocracy shared the new boulevards and parks with elegant tourists and all browsed the wares on display in the new department

5 Die Spitalgasse kurz nach der Elektrifizierung der Tramlinie 1901. – Spitalgasse shortly after the electrification of Berne's tramway in 1901.

6 Der Bahnhofplatz in Bern 1901. Ab 1894 verkehrte in Bern die Dampfstrassenbahn und verdrängte schliesslich den traditionellen Pferdeomnibus. – Berne, Station Square, 1901. From 1894 the city boasted a steam tramway, which eventually replaced the horse buses.

7

8

7 Verkaufs-Magazin im projektierten Geschäfts-Haus des Herrn Baumeister Fasnacht, an der Schauplatzgasse in Bern. Entwurf von Architekt A. Hodler, 1909. – Open-plan shop at Schauplatzgasse in Berne, in the planned commercial building of Mr. Fasnacht, master builder. Sketch by A. Hodler, architect, 1909.

8 Schaufenster des Geschäftshauses Au Bon Marché an der Spitalgasse, 1913. – Shop window of Au Bon Marché department store, Spitalgasse, Berne, 1913.

eröffneten Einkaufspassagen der grossen Warenhäuser. Die bodenständige Beschaulichkeit der Bundesstadt verspürte einen Hauch weltgewandten Flairs europäischer Metropolen wie Paris, Berlin oder London.

Das Hotel Bellevue Palace ist authentischer Ausdruck dieses Lebensgefühls und ein Paradebeispiel der zeitgenössischen Reformarchitektur. Diese umfasst den «Jugendstil», der sich an botanischen und kristallinen Formen orientierte, den «Heimatstil», der Bauwerke und Ausstattungen in der Tradition der jeweiligen Region zu verankern suchte sowie die späteste Ausprägung des Klassizismus, der gern wieder auf Formen den Klassizismus der Zeit «um 1800» zurückgriff.

La belle vie – la belle vue. Warum das Hotel Bellevue «Bellevue» heisst

Reisen in die Schweizer Alpen waren, angeregt durch das 1729 erschienene Gedicht «Die Alpen» des Berner Mediziners, Botanikers und Wissenschaftspublizisten, Dichters und Literaturkritikers Albrecht von Haller, im 18. Jahrhundert sehr in Mode gekommen. Haller hatte darin unter anderem die Älpler als Menschen besungen, die als «edle Wilde» leben, weil sie mit der Zivilisation und allen ihren negativen Begleiterscheinungen noch nicht in Berührung gekommen seien. Jean-Jacques Rousseau hatte mit dem ihm zugeschriebenen Aufruf «Retour à la nature» die Reiselust in die scheinbar noch unberührte wilde Natur intensiviert, und Salomon Gessner öffnete mit seinen «Idyllen» den Blick für eine beschaulich-romantisch verklärte Schönheit der Landschaft und des ländlichen Lebens. In ihrer Nach-

stores and shopping arcades. The down-to-earth Federal capital began to breathe an atmosphere similar to that of any of Europe's great cities – Berlin, London, or Paris.

The Bellevue Palace Hotel is both an authentic expression of this attitude, and an outstanding example of *Reformarchitektur* (Arts and Crafts architecture), which encompasses *Art Nouveau* inspired by botanical and crystalline forms; so-called Regionalism which attempts to locate its buildings and interiors in the various regions; and the latest form of Classicism evoking the Classicism of around 1800.

La belle vie – la belle vue. How the Bellevue Hotel came by its name

In 1729 Bernese polymath – physician, botanist and scientific publicist, as well as a poet and literary critic – Albrecht von Haller published his epic poem, *Die Alpen*. It drew a veritable tourist boom to the Swiss Alps, whose inhabitants von Haller described as «noble savages» who had not (yet) come into contact with civilisation and all its negative side-effects. Both tourism and souvenir sales flourished as Jean-Jacques Rousseau promoted travel with his call of *retour à la nature* while Salomon Gessner and his *idylls* opened travellers' eyes to the charms of the landscape and rural life. Following their example, artists such as Johann Ludwig Aberli, the two Gabriel Lory (father and son) and Niklaus König produced tinted etchings of Bernese landscapes and villages for sale as souvenirs and travel brochures. To the same end, Sigmund Freudenberger created his amusing scenes of rural life, *The noble savage in everyday life*.

folge schufen Johann Ludwig Aberli (Vater), Gabriel Lory (Sohn), Niklaus König und andere handkolorierte Radierungen und Fächer für die Damen der feinen Gesellschaft mit Berner Landschaften und Dörfern und verkauften sie erfolgreich als Souvenir und Reiseprospekt in einem. Sigmund Freudenberger verfasste für den gleichen Zweck seine heiteren Szenen des Landlebens: Die «Edlen Wilden» im Alltag.

Zum Durchbruch des Tourismus im Berner Oberland haben entscheidend die Unspunnenfeste 1805 und 1808 beigetragen. Vier aristokratische Bernburger machten mit der Veranstaltung des ersten Unspunnenfestes 1805 auf dem «Bödeli» oberhalb von Interlaken die Alpenregion mit ihren Naturschönheiten und urchigen Sitten und Gebräuchen international bekannt. Man kündigte das Unspunnenfest 1805 unter anderem im Pariser «Moniteur Universel» und 1808 zudem in der «Gazette de France» an. Die «edlen Wilden» massen sich im Alphornblasen, Schwingen und im Stossen des 83,5 kg schweren Unspunnensteins. Zum zweiten Alphirtenfest im Jahr 1808 waren 5000 Besucher angereist, darunter mehrere hundert von den Initianten persönlich eingeladene adlige Damen und Herren, von der Gräfin bis zum Erbprinzen. Viele Einheimische empfanden das Alphirtenfest eher als Instrument stadtbernischer Machtansprüche. Bei den Besuchern stiessen die Unspunnenfeste jedoch auf stürmische Begeisterung und verankerten das Bild einer weitgehend unberührten, von glücklichen Berglern bewohnten, wilden Landschaft als verlockende Reisedestination weit über die Landesgrenzen hinaus. Germaine de Staël widmete dem Schweizerischen Alphirtenfest

Among the decisive events that really put the Bernese Oberland on the tourist menu were two major Alpine events, the Unspunnen festivities of 1805 and 1808. Four *Bernburger* [aristocratic citizens of Berne] organised the first *Unspunnenfest* of 1805 below the castle ruin of Unspunnen on Interlaken's *Bödeli,* an alluvial plain between the lakes of Thun and Interlaken. Their intention was to celebrate the natural splendours of the Bernese Alps and the quaint rustic customs of the mountain folk, and to ensure international attention and attendance. The 1805 event was advertised in the Paris *Moniteur Universel*, for example, and the 1808 edition was also mentioned in the *Gazette de France*. The «noble savages» competed against one another in Alphorn playing, *Schwingen* – a kind of wrestling – and in throwing the *Unspunnenstein*, a large egg-shaped piece of rock weighing 83.5 kilogrammes (over 13 stone). The second *Unspunnenfest*, held in 1808, drew five thousand spectators, many of them from afar. Several hundred attended as the initiators' personal guests, and included a future king, a countess and other members of the aristocracy. While many locals saw these festivities as demonstrations of power imposed on them by Berne's potentates, the visitors welcomed them enthusiastically. In the minds of people living far beyond the country's borders, the Unspunnen festivities implanted as an alluring tourist destination the image of a largely pristine, wild landscape inhabited by care-free mountain folk. In her travel accounts, *de l'Allemagne*, Germaine de Staël dedicated a chapter of its own to the *Unspunnenfest* of 1808, which she attended in the company of French painter Elisabeth Vigée-Lebrun. As a memento of the «most beautiful

9 Das Alphirtenfest in Unspunnen am 17. August 1808. Ölgemälde von Marie Louise Elisabeth Vigée-Lebrun 1808/09. – Oil painting by Marie Louise Elisabeth Vigée-Lebrun, 1808/09, depicting the alpine festival held at Unspunnen on 17th August 1808.

10 Selbstporträt der französischen Malerin Marie Louise Elisabeth Vigée-Lebrun. 1782. – The French painter, Marie Louise Elisabeth Vigée-Lebrun. Self-portrait, 1782.

von 1808, welches sie in Begleitung der Malerin Elisabeth Vigée-Lebrun besuchte, in ihrem Buch «de l'Allemagne» ein eigenes Kapitel. Die französische Künstlerin malte als Erinnerung an den «schönsten Anblick, den sie je gesehen hatte» das bunte Treiben am Älplerfest unterhalb der Ruine Unspunnen vor der eindrücklichen Bergkulisse. Vigée-Lebrun liess das Ölbild als «Werbung» sogar in einem Pariser Salon ausstellen. Zudem pries Germaine de Staël in ihren Schilderungen insbesondere die Schönheiten und Vorzüge der Stadt Bern für die Reisenden.[3] Der Zwischenhalt in Bern wurde zunehmend zu einem «must» auf dem Weg ins vielgerühmte Berner Oberland.

Wenn im 18. Jahrhundert Touristen auf ihrer Reise ins Oberland vermehrt in Bern im «Adler» oder in der «Krone» abstiegen, hielten sie in der unteren Altstadt vergeblich Ausschau nach ihrem Reiseziel, den Alpen. Standen sie auf der Plattform vor dem Münster, verdeckte das damals noch unbebaute Kirchenfeld die Aussicht auf die verschneiten Bergketten – die Altstadt liegt zu tief im Aarebogen. Erst 1810–1814 – nach den Erfolgen der ersten Unspunnenfeste – liess die Berner Obrigkeit einen öffentlich zugänglichen Ort in der Stadt schaffen, von wo aus Einheimische und auswärtige Besucher bei gutem Wetter eine unvergleichliche Aussicht auf die imposante Alpenkette geniessen konnten: Innerhalb des Oberen Marzilitors, dort wo die Haldenmauer des Gerberngrabens bei der Berner Münzstätte auf den Marzilirain traf, baute Johann Daniel Osterrieth die halbrunde Münzterrasse. Der attraktive Aussichtspunkt erhielt bald den Namen «Belvédère» oder «Bellevue».

sights I have ever seen», Vigée-Lebrun painted in lively oils the comings and goings at the festival against the awe-inspiring backdrop of the Alps. What's more, Vigée-Lebrun «advertised» the event when she put her oil painting on display in a Paris salon. Germaine de Staël's accounts moreover praised the beauty and amenities to travellers of the city of Berne.[3] It rapidly became *de rigueur* to break one's journey to the fabled Bernese Oberland by spending a day or so in Switzerland's capital city.

In the 18th century, increasing numbers of tourists on their way to the Oberland stopped off at the Adler or Krone, two hotels situated in the lower part of Berne's Old City that descends to the oxbow of the Aare river. There they searched in vain for a glimpse of the Alps, their destination. The view from the Cathedral terrace was obstructed by the woodlands of the – as yet undeveloped – Kirchenfeld district. It was not until 1810–1814 – several years after the first Unspunnen festivals – that the Bernese authorities created an publicly accessible area in the city, which in fine weather proffered a view of the entire Alpine range: near the Bernese Mint Johann Daniel Osterrieth was commissioned to build a semi-circular viewing platform, the Münzterrasse, inside the gateway called Oberes Marzilitor, where the medieval Haldenmauer curtain wall rises from Gerberngraben to meet the steep Marzilirain. The new viewing platform soon received the name of *Belvédère* or *Bellevue*.

11

12

11 «Panorama depuis la terrasse de la monnoye à Berne. Panorama der Münzterrasse in Bern». Um 1824. – Panorama from the Münzterrasse in Berne, ca. 1824.

12 Der Blick vom Schwellenmätteli hinauf zur Berner Münzstätte; davor die Aussichtsplattform «Belvédère» oder «Bellevue», die dem hier gebauten Hotel den Namen gab. Gouache von 1815 von Christoph Rheiner. – View from Schwellenmätteli up to the Bernese Mint; in the foreground, the viewing terrace called *Belvédère* or *Bellevue*, which was to give the later hotel its name. Gouache by Christoph Rheiner, 1815.

Der Vorgängerbau. Das Hotel Bellevue von 1864–1865
The Predecessor Building, or the old Bellevue Hotel

Ein Blick in die Geschichte

Nachdem die letzte Tagsatzung am 14. September 1848 in Bern die Bundesverfassung für angenommen erklärt hatte und am 6. November 1848 die nach der neuen Verfassung gewählten Eidgenössischen Räte in Bern zu ihrer ersten Session zusammengetreten waren, bestimmten sie Bern zur Bundesstadt, zum Sitz der Bundesbehörden. Das bedeutete, dass neben dem Bundesrat und der neu zu schaffenden Verwaltung, die es in der alten Eidgenossenschaft nicht gegeben hatte, auch die damals 111 National- und 44 Ständeräte einige Male pro Jahr für längere Zeit zu den Parlamentssessionen nach Bern kommen würden. Nun galt es, die notwendige Infrastruktur bereit zu stellen. Als nach recht zähen Verhandlungen zwischen dem Bundesrat und der Stadt Bern 1850 feststand, dass das Bundes-Rathaus an der Südkante der oberen Altstadt und nicht – wie dies der Bundesrat gewünscht hatte – auf der Grossen Schanze errichtet werden sollte, handelte Jean Kraft, der Wirt des Hotels «Krone» an der Gerechtigkeitsgasse, als Erster. Er liess 1856–1858 von Friedrich Studer und Johann Carl Dähler auf der Westseite des Bundes-Rathauses das Hotel «Bernerhof» errichten, auf das er sein Patent der «Krone» übertrug.

A Glance at History

On 14th September 1848 the last Diet in Berne adopted the Federal Constitution; on 6th November the Federal Assemblies, freshly elected in accordance with the new Constitution, convened in Berne for their first session. They chose Berne as the Federal capital and seat of the Federal authorities. This meant that, in addition to the Federal Council and the administration, which had not existed in the old Confederation and was yet to be created, the then 111 national councillors and 44 councillors of states would be coming to Berne several times a year for relatively long stays during the parliamentary sessions. It was now time to provide the necessary infrastructure.

The Federal Council had wished for the new Federal State House to be constructed at the *Grosse Schanze* [Large Bastion]. In 1850, fairly tough negotiations between the Federal Council and the city authorities, however, led to the decision that it should be located at the southern edge of the upper Old City.

Jean Kraft, the landlord of the Krone Hotel in Gerechtigkeitsgasse, was the first to respond to this decision by commissioning Friedrich Studer and Johann Carl Dähler for the

13

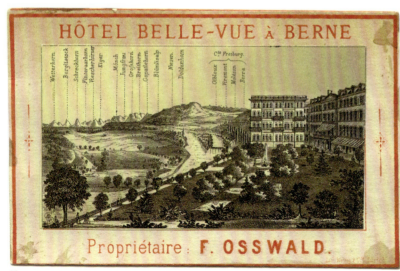

14

BERN (543 M. ü. M.) **HOTEL BELLEVUE**
Prachtvolle Lage mit wundervoller Aussicht auf die Alpen. 85 Zimmer, 115 Betten, Lese- u. Rauchzimmer, Damensalon, Bibliothek, grosse Terrasse, Personen-Aufzug, elektrisches Licht, Telephon, Bäder, Douchen, Luftheizung, Garten. Omnibus am Bahnhof. Die Besitzerin: **Wwe. Osswald.**

	Preis pro Person und pro Tag	
Geöffnet: Das ganze Jahr	15. Juli bis 15. Sep. Fr.	Uebr. Zeit Fr.
Zimmer m. 1 Bett	4–8	4–8
" " 2 "	8–14	8–14
(ausgenommen Appartementszimmer)		
Beleuchtung	i. Zimmerpreis inbegriffen	
Bedienung		
Heizung	2.— per Korb	
Privatsalon	8–20	
Frühstück compl.	1.50	Winter
I. T. d'hôte o. W.	3.—	4.50
II. T. d'hôte o. W.	4.50	3.—
Pension mit Zim.	10–15	8–13
Omnibus	—.75	—.75
Trinkgeld	n. Belieben	

Pensionspreise bei mindestens 8 Tagen Aufenthalt. Kinder bis zu 10 Jahren geniessen 1/3–1/2 Ermässigung. Dienerschaft: Fr. 5 ohne Zim.

BERN (543 M. ü. M.) **HOTEL BERNERHOF**
Steht von allen Seiten frei, in schönster Lage mit voller Alpen-Ansicht, zwischen Bundespalast und Schanzenpromenade. 120 Zimmer, 150 Betten, Lese- und Rauchzimmer, Damensalon, Bibliothek, Terrasse, Lift, elektr. Licht, Telephon, Bäder, Niederdruckheizung. Omnibus am Bahnhof. Die Besitzer: **Kraft & Wieland.**

	Preis pro Person und pro Tag	
Geöffnet: Das ganze Jahr	15. Juli bis 30. Sep. Fr.	Uebr. Zeit Fr.
Zimmer m. 1 Bett	4.50–8	4–7
" " 2 "	7–16	6–12
(ausgenommen Appartementszimmer)		
Beleuchtung	i. Zimmerpreis inbegriffen	
Bedienung		
Heizung	—.75 per Bett	
Privatsalon	12–25	8–15
Frühstück compl.	1.50	1.50
I. T. d'hôte o. W.	4.—	3.50
II. T. d'hôte o. W.	5.—	5.—
Pension mit Zim.	keine	11–14
Trinkgeld		
Omnibus	—.75 p. Pers.	

Pensionspreise bei mindestens einer Woche Aufenthalt. Kinder bis zu 10 Jahren zahlen halbe Preise. Dienerschaft: 5 Fr. ohne Zim.

15

J'ai l'honneur de prévenir mes amis et messieurs les voyageurs que j'ai quitté le Faucon le 2 de ce mois et qu'en attendant que mon nouvel **Hôtel Bellevue** soit prêt, je les recevrai dans la maison vis-à-vis. Ils trouveront mon omnibus à la gare à l'arrivée de chaque train.

Berne, le 2 février 1865
306   F. OSSWALD.

16

13 Südfront der Stadt Bern mit dem Grandhotel Bernerhof (links), dem Bundes-Rathaus, dem Alten Inselspital und dem Westflügel des Hotels Bellevue. Dahinter ragt der Turm des Berner Münsters empor. Aufnahme vor 1888. – The southern aspect of Berne, with Grand-hotel Bernerhof (left), the Federal State House, the old Insel Hospital and the west wing of the Bellevue Hotel, behind which rises the spire of Berne's Münster. Photograph pre-dating 1888.

14 Die Werbekarte zeigt die Bergketten der Freiburger und der Berner Alpen, die kurzerhand vom Osten in den Westen des Hotels versetzt wurden. – The publicity card shows the mountain ranges of the Fribourg and Bernese Alps, transposed from the east to the west of the hotel for visual effect.

15 Hotel Bellevue und Hotel Bernerhof. Aus: Die Hotels der Schweiz. Ein Führer und Ratgeber für Touristen, Basel 1896. – The Hotels of Switzerland. A Guide for Tourists. Basle, 1896.

16 Ankündigung der Eröffnung des Hotels Bellevue, im Journal de Genève, 1865. – Advertisement announcing the opening of the Bellevue Hotel in the *Journal de Genève*, 1865.

Kurz nach der Eröffnung des «Bernerhofs» 1858 packte auch der Wirt des «Falken» an der Münstergasse, Carl Friedrich Leopold Osswald, die Gelegenheit und erwarb am 19. Januar 1864 von den Brüdern Aebi zwei Liegenschaften an der damaligen Inselgasse, zwischen dem alten Inselspital (an seiner Stelle wurde später des Bundeshaus Ost gebaut) und der Berner Münzstätte. Osswald liess hier vermutlich durch den Architekten Gustav Conod,[4] ein stattliches Hotel errichten und benannte es mit cleverem Unternehmerinstinkt nach dem vielbesuchten Aussichtspunkt «Bellevue». 1865 fand die festliche Eröffnung statt.

Die Parzelle an der Inselgasse lag zwischen zwei prominenten Bauten. Westlich grenzte das Haus an, in dem Kaiser Joseph II. 1777 den Berner Universalgelehrten Albrecht von Haller besucht hatte. Auf der Ostseite befand sich die «Münze», die als Berner Münzstätte vom Pariser Architekten Jacques-Denis Antoine 1789–1792 erbaut worden war und seit 1855 als Eidgenössische Münzprägeanstalt diente. Carl Friedrich Leopold Osswald liess sein Hotel mit 110 Gästebetten als zweiflüglige Anlage errichten. Der Haupttrakt erstreckte sich entlang der Inselgasse, der Seitentrakt bildete die Grenze zum Hallerhaus. Die Zimmer blickten alle nach Süden beziehungsweise nach Osten. So konnten die Gäste in praktisch allen Zimmern eine fantastische Aussicht auf die Alpen und auf den besonnten Gartenhof geniessen.

Das 1865 eröffnete «Hotel Bellevue» diente nicht nur den Parlamentariern während der Sessionen, sondern auch einer andern, illustren Klientel: Der damals international bekannte Berner Chirurg und Professor Emil Theodor

construction of the Bernerhof Hotel (1856–1858) to the west of the Federal State House. Moreover, Kraft subsequently transferred his inn-keeper's license to the new hotel.

On 19th January 1864, a few years after the opening of the Bernerhof, Carl Friedrich Leopold Osswald, the Falken landlord in Münstergasse, purchased from the Aebi brothers two properties in Inselgasse, between the Bernese Mint and the old Inselspital, which would eventually be replaced by the East Wing of the Federal Palace. Probably employing the architect Gustav Conod,[4] Osswald commissioned a substantial hotel. His unerring business instinct inspired him to call it *Bellevue*, after the popular viewing point. The new establishment opened in 1865 with great pomp and circumstance.

The plot of land in Inselgasse was sandwiched between two prominent buildings: in the neighbouring house to the west, Albrecht von Haller had once received Emperor Joseph II; to the east was the Bernese Mint, built by Jacques-Denis Antoine in 1789–1792 and in use by the Swiss Federal Mint since 1855. Osswald's hotel was a double-winged complex with 110 beds. The main tract bordered the street, with the west wing adjacent to Albrecht von Haller's house. All the guest rooms faced south and east, affording lovely views of the Alps and the sunny courtyard garden.

The then new hotel was not only frequented by parliamentarians during their sessions but also by other illustrious clients. Bernese surgeon, professor and 1909 Nobel Prize winner for medicine, Emil Theodor Kocher, had been performing surgical interventions in Berne since 1866. At the original Inselspital, which was on the site of what is now

Die Familie Osswald

Carl Friedrich Leopold Osswald (1816–1883), gebürtig aus Offenburg im Grossherzogtum Baden, erwarb sich sein Renommee als führender Hotelier im Gasthof «Goldener Falken», den er gemeinsam mit Anton Schäuble seit 1845 in Pacht genommen hatte (beide waren bis zum Antritt der Pacht im «Goldenen Falken» als Kellner und Buchhalter im Gasthof «Drei Könige» in Basel tätig gewesen). Der «Goldene Falken» – seit 1722 gleichzeitig das Zunfthaus zu Mittellöwen – galt seit der frühen Neuzeit neben der «Krone» als erstes Haus am Platz.

1850 ehelichte Osswald Maria Antonia Philippine Schäuble (1825–1896) aus Waldshut, die Schwester seines Mitpächters im «Goldenen Falken». Das Paar hatte vier Kinder, zwei Töchter und zwei Söhne, welch letztere beide in die Fussstapfen des Vaters treten sollten:
– Maria Antonia Philippine (*1852); sie heiratete 1872
  Joseph August Wilhelm Kottmann aus Solothurn
– Emma Sophie (*1855); 1876 vermählte sie sich mit
  August Joseph Rosenthal aus Mannheim
– Friedrich Anton Alphons (1857–1900), ledig, Hotelier
– Carl Georg Philipp (1863–1918), ledig, Hotelier

Bereits im Jahre 1865 hatte der Vater Carl Friedrich Leopold Osswald für sich und seine Familie das Berner Burgerrecht erworben, sie wurden zünftig auf Schmieden.

Nach dem Tod des Vaters führte die Mutter, unterstützt durch einen Direktor, mit den beiden Söhnen das Haus weiter. Carl Georg Philipp Osswald brachte 1911 die Liegenschaft als Anteil der Familie in die Aktiengesellschaft Hotel Bellevue Palace AG ein und zog sich anschliessend aus der Leitung des Hotels zurück.

The Osswald family

Carl Friedrich Leopold Osswald (1816–1883), a native of Offenburg in the Grand Duchy of Swabia, Germany, became renowned as a leading hotelier in the Falken, which he had taken over as landlord together with Anton Schäuble in 1845 (before acquiring the lease of the Goldener Falken, they had both worked at the *Drei Könige Hotel* [Three Kings Hotel] in Basle, as a waiter and bookkeeper respectively). Since early modern times the Goldene Falken – also the *Zunfthaus zu Mittellöwen* since 1722 – had been regarded as the city's best hotel besides the Krone.

In 1850 Osswald married the sister of his fellow-landlord at the *Goldene Falken*, Maria Antonia Philippine Schäuble (1825–1896) from Waldshut. The couple had two daughters and two sons; the latter were both to follow in their father's footsteps:
– Maria Antonia Philippine (*1852); in 1872 she married
  Joseph August Wilhelm Kottmann from Solothurn, Switzerland
– Emma Sophie (*1855); in 1876 she was to marry
  August Joseph Rosenthal from Mannheim, Germany
– Friedrich Anton Alphons (1857–1900), single, hotelier
– Carl Georg Philipp (1863–1918), single, hotelier

In 1865 father Carl Friedrich Leopold Osswald had already acquired Bernese *Burgerrecht* [their rights as Bernese burghers] for himself and his family; they belonged to the Smiths' Guild.

Following the death of her husband, the older Maria Antonia Philippine continued to run the business with her two sons and a manager. In 1911 Carl Georg Philipp Osswald transferred the property to the newly-formed Hotel Bellevue Palace Ltd. as the family's share; he subsequently resigned from the new company's managing board.

17

18

17–19 Mitglieder der Gründerfamilie: Vater Carl F.L. Osswald, Mutter M.A. Philippine Osswald-Schäuble und Sohn C.G. Philipp Osswald. – Members of the founding family: Carl F.L. Osswald (the father), M.A. Philippine Osswald-Schäuble (the mother) and C.G. Philipp Osswald (one of the sons).

19

20 Blick von Osten in die Kochergasse mit der Eingangsfassade des alten Hotels Bellevue. Vor dem Eingang wartet der hoteleigene Pferdeomnibus. Fotografie um 1905. – View of Kochergasse from the east, with main entrance to the old Bellevue Hotel, outside which the hotel-owned horse bus is waiting. Photograph, ca. 1905.

21 Die Postkarte zeigt das alte Hotel Bellevue von der Gartenseite. Links erkennt man den Westflügel, in der Mitte den Haupttrakt und rechts einen Teil der Berner Münzstätte. – The postcard shows the old Bellevue Hotel as seen from the garden. On the left, the west wing; in the centre, the main tract, and on the right, part of the Bernese Mint.

22 Der Speisesaal im alten Hotel Bellevue. Postkarte. – The dining-room in the old Bellevue Hotel. Postcard.

23 Bei Staatsbanketten im alten Hotel Bellevue dürfte es ähnlich festlich zu und her gegangen sein wie 1912 im Bernerhof beim Staatsdîner für Kaiser Wilhelm II. – The state banquets at the old Bellevue Hotel are likely to have been held in similarly elegant fashion as the 1912 state dinner held in honour of German Emperor, William II, at the Bernerhof Hotel.

Kocher operierte seit 1866 in Bern und wurde 1909 «für seine Arbeit über die Physiologie, Pathologie und Chirurgie der Schilddrüse» mit dem Nobelpreis für Medizin ausgezeichnet. Er führte am Inselspital unter anderem erfolgreich rund 6000 Kropfoperationen durch. Das Alte Inselspital stand in unmittelbarer Nähe westlich des Hotels Bellevue. Damit bot sich für zahlungskräftige Patienten die Annehmlichkeit, sich statt im Barockbau des 1717–1724 von Franz Beer von Bleichten jun. erbauten Inselspitals im benachbarten bequemen und modernen Hotel Bellevue pflegen zu lassen. Die Zahl dieser Gäste verringerte sich erst, als auf Kochers Betreiben hin 1881–1884 das neue Inselspital ausserhalb der Stadt gebaut wurde und Kocher selbst – gerade für diese lukrative Patientengruppe – 1909 nahe beim neuen Inselspital an der Schlösslistrasse seine Privatklinik einrichtete.

Das alte Hotel Bellevue war regelmässig auch Bühne für hochkarätige politische und gesellschaftliche Anlässe. Im «Bellevue» stieg die damalige «High Society» ab. Fürsten, Prinzen, russische Grossfürsten, englische Lords und Ladies, der italienische Adel, französische Minister und zahlungskräftige Amerikaner mit ihren Gattinen residierten in den noblen Räumlichkeiten des Berner Grand Hotels und genossen die kulinarischen Köstlichkeiten der vorzüglichen Küche.

Da der Eidgenossenschaft eigene Repräsentationsräume fehlten, empfingen die Bundesräte die offiziellen Gäste in den festlichen Räumlichkeiten der grossen Hotels der Stadt. Im «Bellevue» wurde der französische General Bourbaki einquartiert, nachdem seine Armee im Deutsch-Französi-

the East Wing of the Federal Palace, directly adjacent to the old Bellevue Hotel, Kocher carried out some 6,000 successful goitre operations, among others. What could be more convenient for wealthy patients than to be looked after by the staff of the comfortable, modern Bellevue Hotel next door? The alternative would have been to convalesce in the Baroque hospital built on the site of a monastery in 1717–1724 by Franz Beer von Bleichten the younger. The number of these guests only diminished after 1881–84, when – as a result of Kocher's initiative – the new Inselspital was built in 1909 on the north-western outskirts of Berne.

The old Bellevue Hotel regularly provided a stage for glittering political and social events. Members of high society stayed there, kings and princes, including the Grand Prince of Russia, and English lords and ladies, Italian aristocrats, French ministers, wealthy Americans and their spouses enjoyed the elegant rooms of the Bernese grand-hotel, and the culinary delights of its excellent kitchen.

Owing to a lack of appropriately prestigious rooms of its own, the Swiss Government received guests in Berne's grand-hotels. French General Charles Denis Bourbaki was billeted at the Bellevue during the Franco-Prussian war of 1870–71, his army having crossed into Switzerland at Les Verrières on 1st February 1871 and having been disarmed. In 1874 the Swiss government held a banquet to celebrate the creation of the General Postal Union (latterly the Universal Postal Union). In 1896 the old Bellevue Hotel welcomed a Spanish grandee, the owner of the first motor car to flit through the streets of Berne. It was there also that, in 1907, the Swiss government gave an elegant *déjeuner* to

schen Krieg am 1. Februar 1871 bei Les Verrières die Schweizer Grenze überschritten hatte und entwaffnet worden war. Im «Bellevue» gab der Bundesrat das Bankett für die Weltpostkonferenz zur Feier der Gründung des Weltpostvereins 1874. Hier offerierte der Bundesrat 1907 das Dejeuner zu Ehren des Freiherrn Marschall von Bieberstein, der die offizielle Mitteilung der Thronbesteigung des Grossherzogs Friedrich II. von Baden überbrachte. 1910 präsidierte Minister Grant Duff das Festbankett zur Feier der Thronbesteigung Georg V. von England. Im gleichen Jahr war Frankreichs Präsident Fallières anlässlich seines offiziellen Besuchs in der Schweiz im «Bellevue» Gast.[5] 1896 logierte im Nobelhotel ein spanischer Grande, der Besitzer des ersten Automobils, das in der Stadt Bern herumkurvte.

1883 starb unerwartet Carl Friedrich Leopold Osswald, der Hotelgründer. Er hinterliess seine Gattin Maria Antonia Philippine, die Töchter Maria Antonia Philippine und Emma Sophie und die Söhne Carl Georg Philipp und Friedrich Anton Alphons. Osswald hatte ein Jahr zuvor Friedrich Haerlin, den späteren Besitzer des Hotels Vier Jahreszeiten in Hamburg, als Direktor eingesetzt, so dass der Hotelbetrieb trotzdem weiter laufen konnte. Als 1896 auch Maria Antonia Philippine Osswald starb, führten die Söhne – vor allem Carl Georg Philipp – das Hotel allein weiter, unterstützt vom Küchenchef Max Metz, der 1895 im alten «Bellevue» begonnen hatte und bis 1936 hier wirkte.

In dieser Zeit veränderte sich die Nachbarschaft des Hotels. 1885 kaufte der Bund das barocke Inselspital, um darin oder an seiner Stelle mehr Platz für die Bundesverwaltung zu schaffen. Aufgrund des Architekturwettbewerbs von 1885

honour Baron Adolf, Marschall von Bieberstein, the official bearer of the news of Frederic II of Baden's ascension to the grand-ducal throne. In 1910 English minister Grant Duff presided over a banquet in celebration of King George V's coronation. Also in 1910, French president Clément Armand Fallières stayed at the old Bellevue Hotel during his state visit to Switzerland.[5]

In 1883 hotel founder Carl Friedrich Leopold Osswald died very suddenly, torn from his busy working life, leaving behind his wife Maria Antonia Philippine, their sons Carl Georg Philipp and Friedrich Anton Alphons, and their daughters Maria Antonia Philippine and Emma Sophie. The previous year, in order to ensure the smooth running of the hotel, Osswald had appointed a manager, Friedrich Haerlin, later owner of the *Vier Jahreszeiten* Hotel in Hamburg. In 1896, after the death of Osswald's widow Maria Antonia Philippine, the sons – but chiefly Carl Georg Philipp – continued to manage the hotel, enjoying the support of hotel chef Max Metz, who had begun his career at the Bellevue in 1895 and worked there until 1936.

During that time the neighbourhood of the hotel underwent various changes: in 1885 the Swiss Government purchased the baroque Insel hospital in order to create more space for the Federal administration. As a result of an architectural competition held in 1885 – but against the jury's wishes – the newly-founded Directorate for Federal Buildings (D+B) commissioned the winner of the second prize, Hans Wilhelm Auer, to build the New Federal State House (today's East Wing of the Federal Palace), which he did from 1888 until 1892. In 1894–1902, following the second com-

– aber nicht im Sinne des Preisgerichts – übertrug die damals gegründete Direktion der Eidgenössischen Bauten dem Gewinner des zweiten Preises im Wettbewerb, Hans Wilhelm Auer, den Bau des «Neuen Bundes-Rathauses» (heute Bundeshaus Ost), das 1888–1892 errichtet wurde. Damit stand nur noch das Hallerhaus zwischen dem Hotel Bellevue und dem Bundeshaus.

Auer baute 1894–1902, nach dem zweiten Bundeshaus-Wettbewerb 1891, zwischen die beiden «Bundes-Rathäuser» auch das Parlamentsgebäude und schuf damit den eindrücklichsten Regierungssitz eines Kleinstaates in Europa.

Die Diskretion und die gediegenen Räumlichkeiten des Hotels – nur wenige Schritte abseits des grellen Rampenlichts des Bundeshauses – schienen wie geschaffen dafür, in anregender Umgebung kreative Verhandlungslösungen zu finden oder politische Allianzen zu schmieden. Hier konnten zudem Staatsoberhäupter angemessen empfangen und einquartiert, Staatsverträge unterzeichnet oder hochrangige Diplomaten mit glanzvollen Diners beeindruckt werden. Das alte «Bellevue» etablierte sich als erstes Haus am Platz. Der Erfolg führte den Hotelbetrieb bald an die Grenzen seiner Platzkapazitäten und seiner Leistungsfähigkeit.

petition for the Parliament building in 1891, Hans Wilhelm Auer was commissioned again, for the Parliament building between the two Federal State Houses. He thus created the most impressive seat of parliament to be seen in a small European state.

The discretion and elegance of the grand-hotel – in the immediate vicinity to, yet at arm's length of the relentlessly glaring lights that shine on the Federal Palace – seemed to be created just to provide a stimulating setting for the search for creative negotiations and solutions, or for the forging of political alliances. In the generously proportioned parlours and salons of the old Bellevue Hotel, heads of state could enjoy the kind of reception and accommodation that befitted their station; treaties could be signed; high-ranking diplomats could be impressed with splendid dinners. The old Bellevue soon became Berne's top establishment. Equally soon, however, its success was to take the hotel to the limits of its capacities, both in terms of space and performance.

25 Ausblick vom Hotel Bellevue auf die Bergkette der Berner Alpen mit Eiger, Mönch und Jungfrau. Um 1935. – View from the Bellevue Hotel of the Bernese Alps with Eiger, Mönch und Jungfrau. Ca. 1935.

24 Blick auf das alte Hotel Bellevue kurz vor dem Abbruch, 19. Sept. 1911. – View of the old Bellevue Hotel shortly before its demolition on 19th September, 1911.

26 «Palais Fédéraux – Bellevue-Palace». Ansicht der Stadtfront von Südosten. Abbildung aus dem Projektbeschrieb 1910. – View of the city from the southeast. Illustration from project description 1910.

27 Protokoll der Gründungsversammlung der Aktiengesellschaft Bellevue Palace vom 7. Oktober 1911. – Minutes of the Founding Assembly of the Bellevue Palace shareholding company, 7th October, 1911.

28 Kumulative Vorzugsaktie der 1911 gegründeten Aktiengesellschaft Bellevue-Palace Grandhotel und Bernerhof, Ausgabe 1923. – Cumulative preferential share of Bellevue Palace Grand-Hotel and Bernerhof, Ltd.; 1923 issue.

Der Bau des Hotels Bellevue Palace 1911–1913
Construction of the Bellevue Palace Hotel

Die Gunst der Stunde genutzt

1911 gründete Carl Georg Philipp Osswald zusammen mit weiteren Interessierten die Hotel Bellevue Palace AG und übertrug ihr das Eigentum am Hotel. Im Verwaltungsrat der Gesellschaft wirkten u. a. Alfred Allaman, Notar in Lausanne und Direktor des Hotels Breuer in Montreux, als Präsident und J. Schieb, Restaurateur des Bahnhofbuffets Bern und Direktor des Kurhotels Gurnigelbad. Sie kauften sofort die Nachbarliegenschaften des Hotels, erwarben das Hallerhaus auf der Westseite und übernahmen von der Eidgenossenschaft die ehemalige Berner Münzstätte auf der Ostseite, für die der Bund im Kirchenfeld Ersatz geschaffen hatte. Die Aktiengesellschaft betraute das Architekturbüro Lindt und Hofmann mit der Planung des Hotelneubaus auf dem ganzen, nun fast doppelt so grossen Terrain. Die Bauarbeiten für das neue Hotel begannen am 1. November 1911 mit dem Abbruch sämtlicher Gebäude auf dem Areal. Am 29. Februar 1912 war der Bauplatz geräumt und für den Neubau bereit.

Für die Zeit bis zur Eröffnung des neuen Hotels richteten Carl Georg Philipp Osswald und sein Küchenchef an der Effingerstrasse, in der Nähe des Kocherschen Privat-

Seizing the moment

In 1911 Carl Georg Philipp Osswald, together with other interested parties, founded Hotel Bellevue Palace Ltd., transferring ownership of the hotel to the new company. On the board of directors were Alfred Allaman, presiding, notary public in Lausanne and manager of the Breuer Hotel in Montreux, and also J. Schieb, proprietor of Berne's Stationsbuffet, the train station restaurant, and manager of the Gurnigelbad spa hotel.

They at once purchased the properties adjacent to the hotel, i.e. the von Haller House to the west, and – from the Federal administration – the former Bernese Mint to the east side, for which the Federal Government had built a replacement in the Kirchenfeld district. The limited company commissioned Lindt and Hofmann architects to design the new hotel building, which was to be constructed on the plot about twice the size of the original hotel. Work on the new building began on 1st November 1911 with the demolition of any buildings remaining on the site, which was completed on 29th February 1912.

For the duration of the construction period, C. G. Philipp Osswald and his chef set up a Hotel Bellevue en miniature

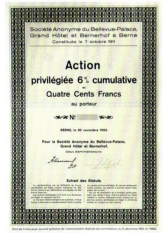

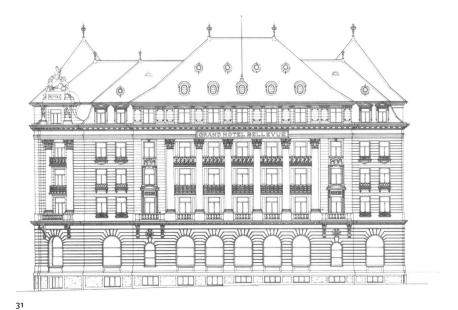
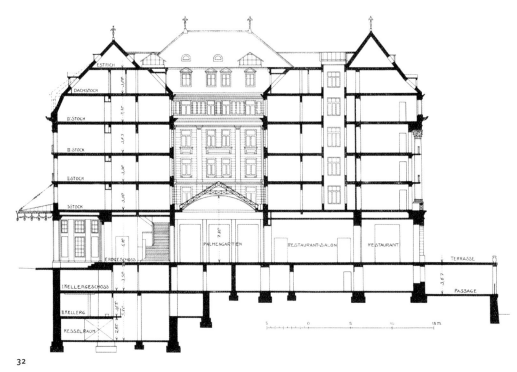
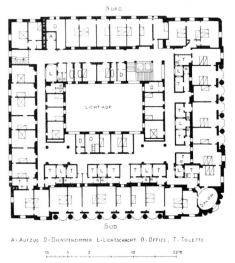

29–32 Grundrisse Erdgeschoss und Obergeschosse, Querschnitt und Ostfassade des Hotels Bellevue Palace. Eingabepläne 1911. – Floor plans, cross section and the east elevation of the Bellevue Palace Hotel. Drawings submitted to planning permission hearings in 1911.

spitals, das «Hotel Bellevue en Miniature» ein, damit sie dort ihre «Kurgäste» weiterhin empfangen konnten.

Stahlbetonskelett und Klimaanlage – In Rekordzeit gebaut und technisch auf dem neusten Stand

Am 1. März 1912 begann man mit dem Neubau. Bereits am 30. November 1912, nach nur neun Monaten, war der Rohbau fertiggestellt und man feierte Aufrichte. Die Konstruktion eines Stahlbetonskeletts ermöglichte diese ausserordentlich kurze Rohbauzeit. Selbstverständlich konnte sich vor dem Ersten Weltkrieg noch niemand einen repräsentativen Hotelbau in Sichtbeton vorstellen. Die gewählte Bauweise, ein Betonskelett mit traditionellen Fassaden aus Haustein und verputztem Mauerwerk, war zwar seit etwa 1895 durchaus üblich. Neu war 1912 aber, dass im neuen «Bellevue» nicht nur die tragenden Bauteile aus Stahlbeton ausgeführt wurden, sondern als Besonderheit auch die Dachkonstruktion. Man wollte so den grösstmöglichen Schutz vor einem Hotelbrand erreichen. Das Stahlbetonskelett bot aber noch einen weiteren Vorteil: Zwischen dem Skelett und der Architektur (nach aussen und nach innen) entstanden fast zwangsläufig Hohlräume. Diese Konstruktion erlaubte den Einbau einer ausgeklügelten Haustechnik auf dem aktuellsten technischen Stand und bot ausreichend Platz für die zahlreichen Steig- und Fallrohre der Wasser- und Abwasserleitungen, für die elektrischen Leitungen, für die Heizung und die Lüftung. Damit konnte das «Bellevue Palace» alle Bequemlichkeiten bieten, die seine Gäste in einem Grandhotel erwarteten. Die 200 Zimmer verfügten über fliessendes Kalt- und Warmwasser und waren mit

close to Kocher's private hospital in Effingerstrasse to be able to continue receiving their privileged *clientèle*.

The new building with its concrete skeleton and air-conditioning – state-of-the-art and built in record time

Work on the new building commenced on 1st March 1912. The «shell» was completed by 30th November of the same year, when the topping-out ceremony was held. By using a reinforced steel skeleton, the builders were able to complete the raw construction in a record time of nine months. Before the First World War, of course, no prestigious hotel building would have been allowed to feature exposed concrete. The method of construction chosen, a concrete skeleton with traditional façades in ashlar and plastered masonry, had been quite common since about 1895. In 1912, however, it was an innovation to execute in reinforced concrete not only the building's load-bearing parts but also the roof construction. The point was to minimise any fire hazards. Another advantage of this method were the inevitable cavities between the skeleton and the architecture, both exterior and interior.

The construction method permitted the installation of sophisticated, then state-of-the-art building technology. The cavities afforded ample space for the numerous standpipes and drains for drinking and waste water, as well as electrical wiring, and heating and ventilation ducts. This enabled the Bellevue Palace to provide all the amenities expected of a grand-hotel. Each of its two-hundred rooms had private toilets with running cold and hot water and modern water closets whose water-filled U-bends kept unpleasant odours

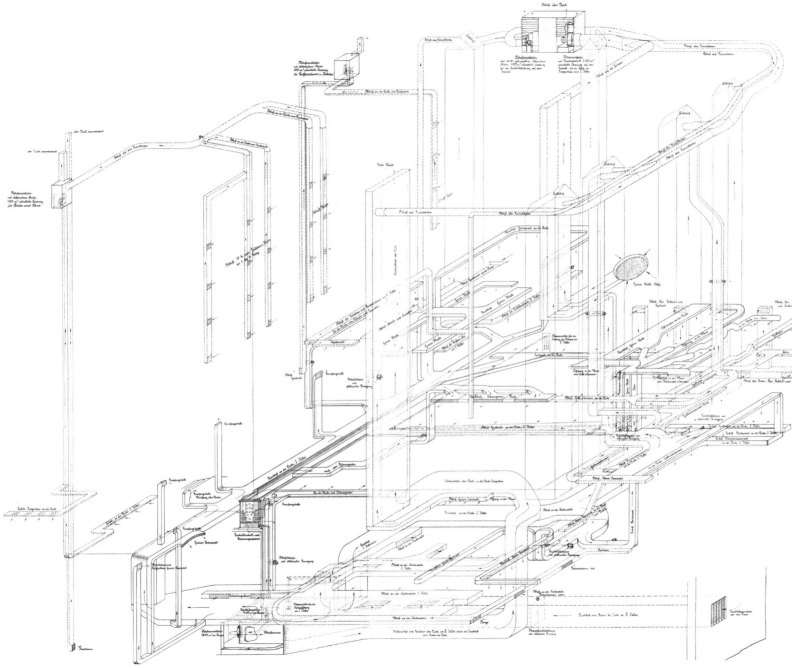

33–34 Ein ausgeklügeltes Heizungs- und Lüftungssystem sorgte für ein angenehmes Raumklima in sämtlichen Räumen des Hotels. Die Steuerung der komplexen Anlage erfolgte über eine zentrale Schalttafel im Hotelbüro. – Controlled from a single panel located in the hotel offices, the complex central heating and ventilation system guaranteed a pleasant ambiance throughout the hotel.

35

36

37

38

35 Die ehemalige grosse Hotelhalle (Salon Royal). Aufnahme aus der Bauzeit. – The former great hotel lobby (Salon Royal). Photograph dating from the time of construction.

36–38 Im Rohbau des neuen Hotels 1912: Die grosse Halle mit Lüftungskanälen und Heizungsleitungen. – Blick vom zukünftigen Speisesaal gegen den Innenhof. Die Rahmenbinder aus armiertem Beton haben eine Spannweite von 13,33 m. – Die Dachkonstruktion mit Kehlgebälk und Lukarnen ist ebenfalls aus armiertem Beton.

Interior of the structural shell of the new hotel, 1912: The Great Hall with ventilation shafts and heating pipes. – View of the interior courtyard from what will be the dining-room. The reinforced concrete frames have a span of 43.73 ft (13.33 m). – Roof structure with collar beams and dormer windows, also of reinforced concrete.

modernen Water Closets mit wassergefülltem Siphon als Geruchsbarriere ausgestattet. Sie erhielten Telefone mit Haus- und teilweise mit direktem Aussenanschluss. Von einer Schalttafel des Hotelbüros aus wurden über ein komplexes Reguliersystem mit Fernthermometern und Manometer Lufttemperatur, Heizwassertemperatur und Dampfdruck sowie die Belüftung und Ventilation des ganzen Hauses gesteuert. Die Heizung war mit einer automatischen Temperaturregelung versehen und zusätzlich noch in verschiedene Heizgruppen aufgeteilt. Diese berücksichtigten Nord- oder Südlage der Zimmertrakte, unterschieden zwischen Gäste- und Wirtschaftsräumen und konnten sogar geschossweise eingestellt werden. Grösste Aufmerksamkeit schenkte man der künstlichen Belüftung und Entlüftung. Die weitverzweigten Lüftungskanäle wurden von den Architekten diskret in Zwischendecken, Wandschränken usw. versteckt, sodass sie für die Gäste nirgends sichtbar waren. Man berechnete 49 000 m³ Frischluftzufuhr pro Stunde – für Toiletten und Bäder stündlich dreimaligen Luftwechsel. Im Sommer wurde die Raumluft gekühlt. Als technisches Highlight hatte man ursprünglich sogar den Einbau einer Luftwaschanlage ins Auge gefasst.[6]

Das Jahr 1913 war ausgefüllt mit dem aufwendigen Innenausbau. Nun erst erhielt das neue Haus sein Gesicht und seine eigentliche Ausstrahlung. Nicht nur Stuck und Wandmalereien, Teppiche, Möbel, Einbaubäder und Lampen, sondern sogar Schrankbeleuchtungen, die sich beim Öffnen der Schranktüren von selbst einschalteten, fehlten nicht.

Mitten in dieser hektischen Arbeitsphase kam am 15. Juni 1913 der Senior des Architekturbüros, Paul Lindt, bei einem

at bay. Each guest room also had a telephone connection to the hotel switchboard; some even had direct external lines. A complex monitoring system located in the hotel's management premises allowed the air temperature, the temperature and pressure of the central heating system, and of the ventilation of the entire building to be regulated by means of remote thermometres and manometres. The heating furnace was equipped with automatic temperature controls; the system consisted of several sections that made allowances for the north or south aspect of the rooms, distinguished between rooms for guests, management, housekeeping etc., and could even be regulated floor by floor. Painstaking attention was given to mechanical ventilation. The architects discreetly concealed the vast network of ventilation shafts above dropped ceilings, behind wall cupboards and elsewhere so that they would remain invisible to the guests. The ventilation system supplied 49,000 cubic metres of fresh air per hour and the air in toilets and bathrooms was fully exchanged every twenty minutes. In summer, the ambient air was cooled. As a technological non-plus-ultra, the original designs even called for the installation of an air-rinsing system.[6]

1913 was devoted to the interior, giving the new hotel its appearance and flair. Work included murals and ornamental plaster, carpets, furniture, built-in baths and lamps – even wardrobe lighting that switched on automatically when the wardrobe door was opened.

In this very busy construction period, on 15th June 1913, Paul Lindt, senior partner of the architectural team, died in a car accident in Windschlag near Offenburg, Germany.

39-40 Architekt Max Hofmann und Ingenieur Bernhard Terner. – Max Hofmann, architect, and Bernhard Terner, structural engineer.

Die Architekten

Die Teilhaber des Architekturbüros Lindt und Hofmann waren Paul Lindt (1859–1913) und Max Hofmann (1872–1965). Hofmann war 1900 in Lindts Firma eingetreten. Die beiden Architekten ergänzten sich offenbar über einen Altersunterschied von 13 Jahren und über sehr verschiedene Ausbildungswege hinweg ausgezeichnet. Lindt war Schüler des Polytechnikums Stuttgart, Hofmann war in München und Wien ausgebildet worden.

Lindt und Hofmann waren zwischen 1900 und 1913 ein sehr erfolgreiches Architekturbüro. Sie bauten 1901 an der Mittelstrasse in Bern für die frisch gegründeten Schweizerischen Bundesbahnen (SBB) ein Verwaltungsgebäude, 1905 an der Marktgasse in Bern ein Geschäftshaus für die Zunft zu Mittellöwen. Es folgten einige Villen in Bern und – vor allem – 1906–1908 für die Burgergemeinde Bern das Casino am Ende der Kirchenfeldbrücke, oben an der Herrengasse. 1912 begannen sie mit dem Bau des Tiefenauspitals, Berns erstem Krankenhaus im Pavillonsystem. Max Hofmann erweiterte den Spitalkomplex nach 1929 und noch 1942 mit einer neuen Tuberkulose-Station.

Das Büro Lindt und Hofmann besass eine respektable Erfahrung im Gastgewerbebau: 1899 Kurhaus Grimmialp (Lindt mit Albert Gerster). – 1900 2. Preis im Wettbewerb um das Casino Bern. – 1902–1905 Grandhotel Gurnigelbad (dessen Direktor war später Mitglied des Verwaltungsrats der Hotel Bellevue Palace AG). – 1906–1908 Bau des Casinos Bern im Auftrag der Berner Burgergemeinde.

Paul Lindt, Bernburger, hatte nach dem Studium bis 1889 in verschiedenen Ämtern und Büros gearbeitet, bevor er 1890 sein eigenes Atelier eröffnete und sich 1893 Hünerwadel als Partner holte. Zu ihren wichtigsten Bauten gehören 1894 die «Falkenburg» am Falkenhöheweg und 1896 der ehemalige Hauptsitz der Berner Mobiliar an der Schwanengasse in Bern (heute Sitz der Berner Stadtverwaltung).

Max Hofmann stammte aus Winterthur. Er blieb nach seinem Studium an den Technischen Hochschulen in München und Wien zunächst in Wien, bereiste dann die USA und zog 1899 nach Bern, wo er kurz bei Ludwig Mathys arbeitete. Nach dem Tod Lindts scheint er nicht mehr sehr viel gebaut zu haben: 1913 eine Villa an der Berner Hochfeldstrasse in barocken Formen; 1919–1921 baute er in Genf, zusammen mit dem dortigen Atelier Marc und Jean Camoletti, das Hotel National zum Sitz des Völkerbunds (Palais Wilson) um, erneuerte in Montreux und Locarno Hotelbauten und errichtete in Bern Spitaltrakte, Wohn- und Industriebauten.

The architects

Paul Lindt (1859–1913) and Max Hofmann (1872–1965) were partners in the architectural office of Lindt and Hofmann, the latter having joined Lindt's office in 1900. Despite their age difference of thirteen years and their very different professional backgrounds, Lindt and Hofmann seemed to complement each other admirably. Lindt was a product of the Stuttgart Polytechnic, while Hofmann had trained in Munich and Vienna.

Between 1900 and 1913 Lindt and Hofmann were a highly successful partnership. In 1901 they constructed administration buildings for the newly-created Swiss Federal Railways in Mittelstrasse, Berne; in 1905 an office building for a Tanners' Guild, the Zunft zu Mittellöwen, in Marktgasse, Berne; several villas, also in Berne and, most importantly, the Casino for the Bernese *Burgergemeinde* at the top of Herrengasse (1906–1908). In 1912 they began the construction of Tiefenauspital, Berne's first hospital to be built in the pavilion system; Max Hofmann extended the hospital complex after 1929, adding a new tuberculosis ward in 1942.

Lindt and Hofmann could boast of a respectable range of experience in building for the catering trade: 1899 the Grimmialp spa hotel (Lindt together with Albert Gerster). – 1900 2nd prize in the competition for the Casino in Berne. – 1902–1905 The Grand-Hotel Gurnigelbad (a spa hotel whose manager became a leading member of the board of directors of Hotel Bellevue Palace Ltd.). – 1906–1908 construction of the Casino in Berne, commissioned by the Bernese Burgergemeinde.

Having completed his studies in 1889, *Paul Lindt*, a member of the Bernese aristocracy, worked in various offices, and also held a government post; in 1890 he opened his own office and, in 1893, appointed Ernst Hünerwadel as his partner. Among their most important buildings were the *Falkenburg* in Falkenhöheweg (1894) and the former headquarters of Berner Mobiliar (insurance company) in Schwanengasse, Berne (1896, today the seat of Berne's city administration).

Max Hofmann, from Winterthur, studied at the institutes of technology in Munich and Vienna. He initially remained in Vienna after his graduation before travelling around the U.S., and moving to Berne in 1899, where he briefly worked for Ludwig Mathys. He does not appear to have built many more notable buildings after Lindt's death, apart from a baroque-style villa in Hochfeldstrasse, Berne (1913); and, together with the Geneva office of Marc and Jean Camoletti, converting Geneva's Hotel National into the League of Nations' headquarters (Palais Wilson, 1919–1921). He also renovated hotels in Montreux and Locarno, and was responsible for hospital, residential and industrial buildings in Berne.

Autounfall in Windschlag bei Offenburg (Deutschland) ums Leben. Jetzt lag die ganze Verantwortung für die Fertigstellung auf den Schultern seines Büropartners Max Hofmann. Er brachte zusammen mit Bauführer Adolf Kies aus Basel den Bau termingerecht zum erfolgreichen Abschluss und rechnete mit 3 255 923.50 Franken ab. Der Kostenvoranschlag hatte 3 275 000.00 Franken vorgesehen. Die Baukosten inklusive Möblierung, Erwerbung der abgetragenen Bauten usw. beliefen sich auf die stolze Summe von 5,8 Millionen Franken. Der Verwaltungsrat berief Fritz Eggimann, der das Kurhaus Bad Weissenburg im Simmental führte, zum ersten Direktor des «Bellevue Palace». Am 27. November 1913 eröffnete das «Bellevue Palace».

Die Neue Zürcher Zeitung würdigte am 2. Dezember 1913 die Eröffnung des jüngsten Luxushotels: «Die Stadt Bern hat alle Veranlassung, auf dasselbe stolz zu sein, hat sie doch mit dem Bellevue Palace ein Hotel erhalten, das hinsichtlich seiner Lage und seiner Ausstattung im Schweizerlande seinesgleichen sucht. […] Grösse und Ausdehnung eines solchen Gebäudes und das Raffinement in der Ausstattung seiner Innenräume erschweren unendlich die Erreichung eines Zieles: in den Glanz und die ausgesuchte Bequemlichkeit auch eine gewisse Wärme hineinzutragen. Dem Architekten des Hotels Bellevue-Palace Herrn Hofmann ist es gelungen.»

Das «Adlon von Bern» – Ein Stück Berner «Schokoladenseite»
Der Neubau von 1913 steht auf einer markanten Geländekante, wo das Plateau der Berner Altstadt nach Süden zur Aare und nach Osten zum Gerberngraben hin abfällt.

The entire responsibility now rested on the shoulders of Max Hofmann. Together with building foreman Adolf Kies from Basle he completed the building on schedule and submitted his final statement of account, which came to a total of CHF 3,255,923.50 (slightly below the estimate of CHF 3,275,000). Total construction costs, including purchasing costs of the buildings that were demolished and all furnishings, amounted to the substantial sum of CHF 5.8 million. The board of directors appointed Fritz Eggimann, manager of the Bad Weissenburg spa hotel in Simmental, as manager of the new Bellevue Palace Hotel.

On 2nd December 1913 the *Neue Zürcher Zeitung* commented on its inauguration with these words: «The city of Berne has every reason to be proud, for the Bellevue Palace is an hotel without equal in Switzerland as regards its position and its furnishings. […] the sheer size and expanse of such a building, and the refinement of its interior furnishings render the achievement of one goal infinitely difficult, namely to imbue its glory and exquisite comfort with a certain warmth. Mr. Hofmann, the architect of the Bellevue Palace Hotel, has reached this goal.»

The «Adlon of Berne» – seeing Berne at its best
Sited on a pronounced ledge whence the plateau of Berne's Old City drops down to the Aare river and eastwards to Gerberngraben, the external structure and the internal layout of the new building of 1913 with its sweeping views of Kirchenfeld bridge and the spectacular panorama of the Alps respond both to its prominent urbanistic situation and to its unique topographic location. The duality that now

41–42 Das Hotel Bellevue Palace, das Bundeshaus Ost und das Parlamentsgebäude von Südosten. Detail des Mittelteils. – The Bellevue Palace Hotel, the East Wing of the Federal Palace, and the Federal Palace as seen from the south-east.

Die äussere Gliederung und die innere Raumanordnung antworten auf die spezielle städtebauliche Situation mit der Orientierung zur Kirchenfeldbrücke hin und mit der Blickausrichtung zum Alpenpanorama auf die einzigartige topografische Lage des Hotels. Dieses so selbstverständlich erscheinende Doppelgesicht des «Bellevue»-Baus verursachte den Architekten einiges Kopfzerbrechen. Geschickt und unauffällig überspielen sie den Konflikt des Gebäudes zwischen diagonaler Ausrichtung nach aussen und axialer Reihung der Repräsentationsräume im Inneren.

Die eindrückliche Hauptschaufassade des Hotels, die sich über seine Süd- und seine Ostseite erstreckt, thront in überaus vornehmer Präsenz über der Aare und reiht sich dank ihrer ausgewogenen Gestaltung harmonisch und dennoch als prägnanter Schlusspunkt in die Abfolge der Bundesbauten ein. In die Süd- und die Ostfassade sind gewaltige korinthische Säulen eingestellt, zwischen denen die Balkone vor den vornehmsten Hotelzimmern leicht ausschwingen. Die beiden Fassaden sind allerdings nicht gleich lang. Die Südfassade zieren sieben säulenbegleitete Fensterachsen, die Ostfassade nur deren fünf. Der eilige Betrachter auf der Kirchenfeldbrücke übersieht diesen kleinen Unterschied wegen der perspektivischen Verkürzung der Südfront. Die abgerundete Gebäudeecke ist mit den von Doppelsäulen flankierten, diagonal gestellten Fensterflächen besonders ausgezeichnet und erscheint gleichsam als kraftvoller Bug des edlen Berner Hotel-Flaggschiffs. Hier prangt an prominenter Stelle, direkt oberhalb der Doppelsäulen, der Namenszug «HOTEL BELLEVUE». Im Vergleich architektonisch bescheiden gestaltet sind hingegen die Nordfassade

appears to be quite natural was quite a challenge for the architects but they cleverly and unobtrusively resolved the structural conflict between the building's diagonal exterior and the interior axial sequence of parlours and salons.

The building sits enthroned in great elegance high above the Aare river. With its harmonious design it constitutes an impressive cornerstone to the sequence of government structures. Its elegantly curved corner and two massive Corinthian double columns form the central projection of the hotel's main façade, with Corinthian columns also flanking the gently outward-curving balconies of the most luxurious, south and eastward-oriented rooms. The wings are unequal in length, however, with seven window axes and columns facing south, but only five facing east. Due to the foreshortening of the south face, pedestrians rushing along Kirchenfeld bridge are unlikely to notice the slight difference.

Resembling the prow of a proud flagship, the curved south-east corner of the building is very prominent. From here, directly above the double columns, the bold lettering of HOTEL BELLEVUE proclaims the glory of the top-class establishment. The architectural design of the north and west façades overlooking Kochergasse and the East Wing of the Federal Palace is more modest, and the main access to the hotel in Kochergasse virtually unadorned. Nevertheless, guests can descend from their transport beneath the sheltering cantilever structure of a splendid filigree glass canopy.

An entablature above the third floor separates the façades from the eaves below an attic floor which also provides for

42

gegen die Kochergasse und die Westfassade gegen das Bundeshaus Ost. Die fast schmucklose Eingangsfront empfängt den Hotelgast an der Kochergasse mit einem weit ausragenden, filigran gearbeiteten Glasdach über der Zufahrt zum Hoteleingang.

Ein kräftiges Hauptgesims über dem dritten Stockwerk trennt die Gebäudefassaden von der Dachlandschaft. Über ihm erhebt sich das Attikageschoss, das ermöglicht, dass auch die hier untergebrachten Gästezimmer ohne Abschrägung der Aussenwände gebaut werden konnten. Darüber sitzt ein Mansarddach, das in der Mitte der beiden Hauptteile der Süd- und der Ostfassade durch mächtige Walmdächer durchbrochen ist: Diese Mittelbauten gebärden sich wie übergrosse bernische Landschlösser und verleihen dem Monumentalbau etwas von der patrizischen Vornehmheit Berns. Die Attika der gerundeten Mitte ist mit Urnen und Fahnenstange bekrönt – ein fast überreiches Architekturprogramm, das den Luxusbau deutlich herausstreicht.

Hinter der Flügeltür des Haupteingangs nimmt der aufmerksame Gast überrascht wahr, dass die innere Anordnung der Räumlichkeiten keineswegs den durch das Äussere geweckten Erwartungen entspricht: Der Bau ist ringförmig um den Innenhof gebaut und im Erdgeschoss konsequent axial vom Haupteingang auf der Nordseite zur Aussichtsterrasse im Süden organisiert. In den verglasten Innenhof, den sogenannten «Palmengarten», münden alle Gesellschaftsräume: der Empfangsbereich im Norden, das Restaurant im Süden, die Hotelhalle (heute Salon Royal) im Osten – ursprünglich mit Fenstertüren zur Ostterrasse, die heute mit der Eventlokalität Münz (ehemals Restaurant Zur Münz) überbaut ist

rooms without sloping exterior walls. The attic floor sits below a mansard roof broken up by massive hip roofs in the sector comprising the two main parts of the south and east façades: these central parts of the building somewhat resemble Bernese country estates. The attic storey in the curved central section is crowned by urns and flagpoles – a slightly over-lavish architectural programme which clearly underscores the building's luxurious character.

Having passed through the double doors of the main entrance, the perceptive visitor will be surprised to find that the interior layout does not correspond to expectations raised by the exterior: the interior courtyard constitutes the centre of the building, and is surrounded by concentric structures. On the ground floor, the rooms are aligned along a clear north-south axis from the main entrance (N) to the viewing terrace (S). The Palm Garden with its stained-glass skylight gives access to all public areas, i.e. the reception area to the north, the dining-room (today's Salon du Palais) to the west, the restaurant to the south, and – to the east – the hotel lobby (today's Salon Royal), whence in former times french windows gave access to the East Terrace, which has since been transformed into the Münz event venue (formerly the Restaurant Zur Münz).

In contrast to the above, the layout of the rooms in the corners of the building does correspond to the impact of the façades: the Lounge (today's Salon Rouge) is located behind the central projection between the south and east façades, while a small dining-room (today's Salon Casino) lies between the Restaurant (today's La Terrasse) and the large main dining-room. The East Terrace used to terminate

44

43-44 Blick auf die ursprüngliche Ostfassade und Fassadendetail des Bellevue Palace. – View of the east façade of the Bellevue Palace Hotel.

– und der Speisesaal (heute Salon du Palais) im Westen. Die Verteilung der Räume hinter den Gebäudeecken entspricht aber dem Gewicht der Fassaden: Hinter dem «Mittelrisalit» zwischen Süd- und Ostfassade befindet sich der Salon (heute Salon Rouge), zwischen dem Restaurant La Terrasse und dem grossen Speisesaal (heute Salon du Palais) liegt der kleine Speisesaal (heute Salon Casino). Die Ostterrasse war nach Norden ursprünglich mit einem eingeschossigen Anbau mit Billardzimmer und Bar abgeschlossen. Daneben lag, gegen die Kochergasse, das Schreib- und Lesezimmer (heute die «Bellevue-Bar»). Beide konnten nur von der Hotelhalle (heute Salon Royal) her betreten werden. In der «unattraktiven» Nordwestecke des Gebäudes befand sich bei der Eröffnung die Hotelverwaltung.

Die breite Haupttreppe in der Nordostecke führt zu den Obergeschossen. Die Zimmeranordnung folgt der diagonalen Symmetrieachse der Hauptfassade: Die komfortabelsten Räume und Suiten blicken nach Süden und Osten. Die bei der Eröffnung einfacheren Zimmer, die damals noch keine eigenen Toiletten und Bäder besassen, liegen hinter der Nord- und der Westfassade und gegen den Innenhof, der durch zwei Ruhezonen in der Südwest- und Südostecke Licht in die innenliegenden Korridore gibt.

Das ganze Hotel erweist sich als ein Triumph der Behaglichkeit und des Luxus. Die Gestaltung und Möblierung der Gesellschaftsräume und der Hotelzimmer entsprach den Möglichkeiten und der Erwartung der Bauzeit. Die Schmuckformen im Stil Louis-seize fand man an allen Möbeln und auf allen Dekorationsstoffen. Abgesehen von den Messingbettstellen waren die Möbel mit Edelhölzern

northwards in a single-storey extension with the Billiards Room and Bar. Next door, towards Kochergasse and only accessible from the hotel lobby (today's Salon Royal) was the Reading and Writing Room (today's Bellevue Bar). The offices have always been located in the north-west corner, the building's least attractive part.

The main staircase in the north-east corner and the service lift in the north-west corner provide access to the upper floors. Here, the rooms are organised along the main façade's diagonal symmetrical axis, with the best rooms and suites facing south and east. The plainer rooms, initially without their own bathrooms or toilets, face north and west, or look out over the interior courtyard, which also provides daylight to guest lobbies in the south-west and south-east corners and thence to the internal corridors. The hotel was an architectural triumph, and spoiled its guests with comfort and luxury, including state-of-the-art technical achievements such as central heating, toilets with a U-bend to keep out unpleasant odours (available on the European Continent since ca. 1895), and air-conditioning (available in Switzerland since ca. 1900). In view of the requirements of the new concrete construction, costly structural and domestic engineering, and fairly complex topographical situation, it is not surprising that the building's architectural clarity was somewhat compromised. The interior design and furnishings of public parlours, salons and guest rooms were in keeping with what was available and expected at the time of construction, and were heavily influenced by the Louis XVI style. The solid-brass bedsteads apart, the furniture was veneered in fine wood or varnished with matte dove-grey

46

45

47

50

furniert oder mit taubengrauem Schleiflack überzogen. Die Gästezimmer erhielten Teppichböden. So präsentierte sich das Haus bei der Eröffnung im Herbst 1913 als «Gesamtkunstwerk».

Obwohl man in der Zeit der Reformarchitektur nicht mehr auf eindeutige Formenzitate älterer oder berühmter Vorbildbauten trifft, stand den Architekten des Hotels Bellevue Palace bei der Planung doch ein grosses Vorbild vor Augen: das Hotel Adlon neben dem Brandenburger Tor in Berlin, das 1907 eröffnet worden war und mit seinem Luxus und Komfort sofort Furore machte.

Beide Hotelbauten bilden eine markante Ecke am Ende einer prominenten Baufluchten. Beide Häuser überspielen die architektonische Gliederung ihrer Fassaden mit einer Attika und einem zusätzlichen Stockwerk von Dachfenstern. Nur das Adlon besitzt aber ein als Mezzanin ausgebildetes Zwischengeschoss über dem Erdgeschoss, das die Gesellschaftsräume enthält. Dennoch: Die von den Berner Architekten offensichtlich gesuchte Verwandtschaft zwischen den beiden Hotels ist nicht zu übersehen, und der Ehrentitel «Adlon von Bern» würde dem «Bellevue Palace» wohl anstehen.

Vom Generalsquartier zum Gästehaus der Eidgenossenschaft

Kurz nach der Fertigstellung des «Bellevue Palace» öffnete, im Sommer 1914 (nach Zürich 1883 und Genf 1896) die dritte Schweizerische Landesausstellung in Bern ihre Tore. Besucher aus der ganzen Schweiz und aus den angrenzenden Ländern strömten nach Bern und garantierten Hochbe-

enamel. The guest rooms were carpeted. When it opened in 1913, the hotel was a late-flowering *Gesamtkunstwerk*.

Although *Reformarchitektur* (Arts and Crafts architecture) did away with unambiguous formal quotations of earlier buildings, the designers of the Bellevue Palace Hotel did model their project on the Adlon Hotel, which in 1907 had opened next to Berlin's Brandenburg Gate, and whose great luxury and comfort caused an immediate sensation.

The two hotels constitute distinctive cornerstones at the end of prominent rows of buildings, and gloss over the architectural division of their façades by an attic storey and an extra flight of dormer windows. Only the Adlon, however, can boast a mezzanine above the ground floor for the lounges, salons and function rooms. Nevertheless, the Bernese architects' striving for a semblance between the two buildings is quite evident and the honorary title of «Adlon of Berne» would sit easily with Berne's Bellevue Palace Hotel.

From the General's headquarters to government guest-house

In the summer of 1914, shortly after completion of the Bellevue Palace Hotel, the third Swiss National Exhibition opened its doors in Berne – after Zürich, 1883, and Geneva, 1896. Visitors from all over Switzerland and neighbouring countries flocked to the city, bringing lively trade and fully-booked rooms to the new hotel. It was a most auspicious beginning.

The lights went out in Europe, however, after the assassination in Sarajevo on 28th June 1914 of Archduke Franz Ferdinand of Austria, heir to the Austro-Hungarian throne,

45–47 *Das Berliner Hotel Adlon war möglicherweise das Vorbild für die architektonische Gliederung des Hotels Bellevue Palace. Hotel Adlon Berlin. Postkarte um 1910. – The Adlon Hotel in Berlin may have served as a model for the architectural structure of the Bellevue Palace Hotel. – Luftaufnahme des Hotels Bellevue Palace um 1980. – Blick auf die ursprüngliche Ostfassade des «Bellevue Palace». – Aerial view of the Bellevue Palace Hotel, ca. 1980. – View of the east façade of the Bellevue Palace Hotel.*

trieb und beste Zimmerbelegung auch im «Bellevue Palace». Das Hotel erlebte einen rundum geglückten Start.

Doch einen Monat nach den Schüssen in Sarajevo gingen in Europa die Lichter aus. Die militärischen und politischen Ereignisse, die der Ermordung des österreichischen Thronfolgers Franz Ferdinand durch bosnische Serben am 28. Juni 1914 folgten, führten mit der Kriegserklärung Österreich-Ungarns an Serbien am 28. Juli 1914 zum Beginn des Ersten Weltkriegs. Praktisch von einem Tag auf den anderen blieben die meisten internationalen Gäste aus.

Am 3. August 1914 bestimmte die Vereinigte Bundesversammlung in Bern nach einem kontroversen politischen Seilziehen der Parteien Ulrich Wille zum General der Schweizer Armee. Er bezog mit seinem Generalstab für die Dauer des Ersten Weltkriegs das Hotel Bellevue Palace als Hauptquartier und befehligte die Schweizer Armee von hier aus. 1915 liess sich Wille durch den Bildhauer August Heer und den Maler Ferdinand Hodler in Ton und Öl porträtieren.

«Vom Neuenburger Schokoladenfabrikanten und Hodler-Sammler Willy Russ stammte der Vorschlag, den auf der Höhe seiner Laufbahn stehenden Ferdinand Hodler mit dem Bildnis des Nachfolgers von Dufour und Herzog zu betrauen. ‹Pourquoi pas?› soll der Künstler dazu gemeint haben, ‹le général a une bonne tête, une vraie binette de vieux Suisse›. Anlässlich der ersten Begegnung habe Wille zum Meister geäussert: ‹Ich gestehe Ihnen offen, verehrter Meister, wenn Sie's nicht wären, so hätte ich wirklich keine Zeit!› Worauf Hodler antwortete: ‹Ja, sehen Sie, Herr General, wenn Sie nicht General wären, so würde ich Sie auch nicht malen.› Zum Ergebnis meinte dann das Modell: ‹Scheusslich

by Bosnian Serbs. A mere month later, on 28th July 1914, Austro-Hungary declared war against Serbia. It was to be the beginning of the First World War. Virtually from one day to the next, international guests stayed away from the hotel.

On 3rd August 1914, Switzerland's united Federal Assembly elected Ulrich Wille as General of the Swiss Army and, for the duration of the war, the Bellevue Palace was the headquarters for Wille and his general staff. It was here that painter Ferdinand Hodler portrayed the General in oil and sculptor August Heer produced a bust in clay:

Willy Russ, Neuchâtel chocolatier and Hodler collector, suggested that Ferdinand Hodler, who was at the height of his artistic career, should paint a portrait of the successor to Swiss generals Henri Dufour and Hans Herzog. «Pourquoi pas?,» the artist is said to have replied, «le géneral a une bonne tête, une vraie binette de vieux Suisse». At their first meeting, the General is reputed to have told the master, «I'll be honest, esteemed master: if it was not for you, I really would not have the time.» To which Hodler replied, «Well, you see, dear General, if you were not the General, I would have no reason to paint your portrait.» When shown the result, the sitter exlaimed, «It is hideous ... but a terrific likeness.» Could it have been the General himself who, in spring 1915, commissioned two Bernese photographers, Franz Henn and J. Kölla, to record his sittings at the Bellevue Palace for Hodler and his sculptor colleague, August Heer? At any rate, the photograph from J. Kölla's studio is not without a certain Chaplinesque touch.[7]

The First World War and military occupation also brought a different clientèle to the Bellevue Palace Hotel,

48

48 Signet des neu eröffneten Hotels, 1913. – The emblem of the newly opened hotel, 1913.

49 Die Hotelhalle in ihrem ursprünglichen Erscheinungsbild. Die Aufnahme um 1925 zeigt schön, warum der überdeckte Innenhof noch heute «Palmengarten» heisst. – The 1925 photograph of the original hotel lobby illustrates why the interior courtyard with its stained glass skylight to be called the Palm Garden.

49

… aber furchtbar ähnlich.› Ob es der General war, der im Frühjahr 1915 gleich zwei Berner Fotografen, Franz Henn und J. Kölla, beauftragte, sein Modellsitzen im «Bellevue Palace» für Hodler und den zusätzlich herbeibestellten Bildhauer August Heer in Lichtbildern festzuhalten, bleibt ungewiss. Jedenfalls entbehrt die hier wiedergegebene Aufnahme des Ateliers J. Kölla nicht einer chaplinesken Note.»[7]

Die militärische «Besetzung» des Hotels brachte auch eine andere Klientel. Neben den Schweizer Offizieren verkehrten während des Ersten Weltkriegs vermehrt Diplomaten und Politiker der verschiedenen Kriegsparteien im «Bellevue Palace». Der amerikanische Diplomat Hugh Wilson schilderte die damalige spezielle Atmosphäre in seinem Buch «Lehrjahre eines Diplomaten» folgendermassen: «Feinde stiessen in demselben Fahrstuhl zusammen, trafen sich vor demselben Tisch, um mit dem Portier zu sprechen und assen im gleichen Speisesaal. Der Speisesaal selber hatte strenge und feste Zonen, trotzdem die Grenzen unsichtbar waren. An der einen Seite sassen die Deutschen, Österreich-Ungarn, Türken und andere der Mittelmächte; an der anderen Seite hatten die Alliierten ihre Tische. Dazwischen war eine Art Niemandsland der Neutralen. Dort hatten die Amerikaner gesessen, bis uns nach dem Abbruch der Beziehungen zu Deutschland der Oberkellner feierlich in die alliierte Ecke versetzt hatte.» Die Unterhaltungen verliefen in gedämpftem Flüsterton, da die jeweils entgegengesetzte Seite stets darauf erpicht war, nützliche Informationen aufzuschnappen. «Spione gab es in Hülle und Fülle. Für unsere beschwingte Einbildungskraft fielen die meisten der im ‹Niemandsland› Sitzenden, denen Beziehungen mit beiden

including Swiss army officers and increasing numbers of diplomats and politicians from the various warring parties. U.S. American Hugh Wilson describes the atmosphere at the hotel in his memoirs, *Diplomat between Wars*:

Enemies bumped into one another in the elevator, found themselves at the same desk talking to the concierge, ate in the same dining room. [...] The dining room itself had hard and fast zones, for all that the boundaries were invisible. At one end sat the Germans, Austro-Hungarians, Turks and others of the Central Powers, at the other end the Allies had their tables. In between was a kind of no-man's-land of neutrals. There had sat the Americans until, after our breach of relations with Germany, the head-waiter had solemnly moved us into the Allied Zone.

Conversations were held in low whispers to prevent opposed parties from picking up useful morsels of information.

The place was overrun with spies. To our colored imagination, most of the occupants of ‹no-man's-land› who could have dealings with both sides, fell into this category. There were business men, exiles, mysterious silent gentlemen of hidden purposes. There were exotic-appearing fashionably dressed women who dined alone and maintained a rigidly correct decorum. In addition to the permanent guests at the hotel were nondescript individuals who arrived on errands or were servants employed by the guests.[8]

A special guest arrived from Munich at the Bellevue Palace in June 1919. It was the intellectual, author, lyricist and dandy Rainer Maria Rilke, who was to remain in Switzerland until his death in 1926, repeatedly visiting Berne and always staying at his «favourite» hotel. Two days after

50 General Wille in seinem Hauptquartier im Hotel Bellevue. Bern 1914. – General Wille in his headquarters at the Bellevue Hotel in Berne, 1914.

51 Militärwache vor dem Hoteleingang. Während des Landesstreiks von 1918 waren neben dem Generalstab zusätzliche 200 Soldaten zum Schutz des Generals im Bellevue einquartiert. Aufnahme um 1915. – Military guards outside the main entrance to the hotel. In addition to the General Staff, two hundred soldiers were billetted at the Bellevue Hotel for the protection of the General during the 1918 General Strike in Switzerland.

52 Das Hotel Bellevue diente im Ersten Weltkrieg von 1914 bis 1918 als Generalsquartier: General Ulrich Wille lässt sich in einem der Salons von Ferdinand Hodler (vorn) und August Heer in Öl und Ton porträtieren. – During the First World War, the General of the Swiss army used the Bellevue Hotel as his headquarters. In one of the salons, General Ulrich Wille is being portrayed in oil by Ferdinand Hodler (foreground) and in clay by sculptor August Heer.

Hinter den Kulissen des modernen Groß=Hotels

Von Dr. W. R.

Welche Mannigfaltigkeit herrscht heute in den Einrichtungen zur Unterbringung und Verpflegung derer, die zum Geschäft oder Vergnügen fremde Länder und Städte aufsuchen! In den stillen Winkeln aller Länder gibt es noch so manchen Gasthof, der in Aussehen und Einrichtungen die gute alte Zeit und alte Landessitten verkörpert, in dem ein biederer Wirt regiert, während die Gattin und ein mehr oder weniger hübsches Töchterlein in der Küche wirken und die Gäste bedienen, und das „Personal" aus einem Hausknecht besteht. Durch alle Abstufungen, die den kulturellen, sozialen und wirtschaftlichen Unterschieden und Schichtungen entsprechen, geht es von der Herberge an der Landstraße und dem bescheidenen Dorfgasthaus bis zum modernen Groß=Hotel. Es gibt heute kaum mehr ein Land der Erde, in dem die Pioniere des modernen Wirtschaftslebens und des Fremdenverkehrs ihren Einzug gehalten haben, das nicht den modernen Hotel=Typus, mit den durch das Klima gebotenen Veränderungen, aber im

Atrium oder Vorhalle zu den Gesellschaftssälen.

Grunde den gleichen, erprobten Einrichtungen, aufweise. Diejenigen Länder, deren Hauptstädte zu Brennpunkten des heutigen Wirtschaftslebens gehören, oder durch die um ihrer Naturschönheiten willen der internationale Fremdenstrom flutet, haben das moderne Hotel am höchsten entwickelt. — Eine vollendete Technik und Organisation, tiefes Studium der Ansprüche und Bedürfnisse des reisenden Publikums, die Summierung internationaler Erfahrungen haben die Einrichtungen des Hotels erster Klasse geschaffen. Ein Hotel, das die höchste Stufe dieser Kategorie einnehmen will, muß unter allen Umständen folgende Einrichtungen aufweisen: fließendes kaltes und heißes Wasser in allen Zimmern, eine genügende Zahl von Zimmern mit Bad, Telefonanschluß nach außen in allen Zimmern und eine verhältnismäßig große Zahl öffentlicher Räume. Ein Hotel ohne Halle, ohne fließendes Wasser und Telefonanschluß in den Zimmern und ohne zahlreiche öffentliche Räume, kann ausgezeichnet sein, darf aber nicht den Anspruch erheben, zur obersten Klasse zu gehören. Diese Klassifizierungs=Merkmale sind äußerlicher Natur. In bezug auf kulinarische Darbietungen wird das Hotel ersten Ranges das Vollkommenste und Auserlesenste zu bieten suchen.

Blick in die „Große Halle".

Innerhalb seiner Klasse kann jedes gutgeleitete Hotel nach der Vollendung streben und auch wenn es, geringeren Preisen entsprechend, einer weniger anspruchsvollen Kundschaft weniger Luxuriöses bietet, in Verpflegung und Bedienung vorzüglich sein. Darum hängt im Hotelwesen alles von der Tüchtigkeit der Leitung ab.

Das größte Interesse für den Uneingeweihten bieten natürlich die technischen und organisatorischen Einrichtungen eines Hotels oberster Klasse, wie desjenigen, das hier etwas näher geschildert sein soll: eines schweizerischen Stadthotels, das einen wohlverdienten hohen Ruf genießt.

Es ist selbstverständlich, daß man beim Bau eines solchen Hotels nicht nur architektonisch etwas Gutes zu schaffen strebt, sondern daß dabei auch die letzten Errungenschaften der Technik ihre Anwendung finden, sei es in der Anlage und Verteilung der Räume, sei es hinsichtlich Heizung, Lüftung, Beleuchtung oder in dem so wichtigen Punkte der Fernhaltung der Außengeräusche von den Zimmern! — Der Eintretende findet sich im Atrium, einem vornehmen, behaglichen Raum mit Oberlicht, um sich sämtliche Gesellschaftsräume gruppieren. Es ist ein

Zentral=Office des Servierpersonals.

vorbildlich schöner Empfangsraum. Hier versammeln sich die Gäste vor den Mahlzeiten, von hier geht man den Speise= und Gesellschaftssälen zu. Zur vollen Wirkung verlangt das Atrium das bewegte Leben einer eleganten Menge, ein großes gesellschaftliches Ereignis, wie etwa Besuche ausländischer Fürstlichkeiten, Staatsmänner oder sonstiger führender Persönlichkeiten, zu deren Ehren hier Empfänge stattfinden. Auf der einen Seite des Entrees, gewissermaßen in der Vorhalle des Atriums, wird dem Gaste zuerst die nach dem sogenannten „open desk=System" angelegte Rezeptionsabteilung sichtbar. An diesem rechtwinklig angeordneten langgestreckten Tische meldet sich der ankommende Gast, um sich einschreiben zu lassen. — Die oberen Stockwerke des Hotels sind, auch wenn sie noch so hübsch ausgestattet sein mögen, doch weit weniger interessant, als seine Unterwelt, unter der Halle. Hier, in den Küchenräumen und im Keller, vollzieht sich das, was am meisten zur Festigung des Rufes eines Hotels beiträgt.

Ein großer, heller Raum mit einer Reihe von Nebenräumen, in dem zahlreiche Männer in weißer Jacke und weißer Mütze geschäftig hin und her eilen, das ist sozusagen die Herzkammer des Hotels. Den Mittelpunkt des Hauptraumes nimmt ein mächtiger Tafelherd ein, der Brandopferaltar, an dem der Hohepriester der Gastronomie, der Küchenchef, mit seinen Helfern seines Amtes waltet. Neben dem großen Herd steht ein zweiter, der Restaurationsherd, daneben zwei gewaltige Dampfkochkessel. Im Hintergrund, an der Wand, ist ein Doppel=Grill angebracht, daneben der sogenannte „Salamander", der Gratinier=Apparat, in dem gewisse, auf dem Herde fertiggestellte Speisen ihre letzte, appetitliche Bräunung erfahren. Ein besonderer Herd dient der Zubereitung des Frühstücks, das durch elektrische Aufzüge nach den Etagen befördert wird. In Nebenräumen befindet sich

Privat=Eßzimmer mit 20 Gedecken.

die warme Pâtisserie, mit einem großen Backofen, die kalte Pâtisserie, mit Hilfsmaschinen zum Schneeschlagen, Eisbrechen usw. In der kalten Küche werden die kalten Speisen hergerichtet. Ein großer Fischbehälter mit eigener Quell=Leitung birgt lebende Fische. In anderen Nebenräumen befinden sich die Maschinen zum Tellerspülen, Silberpolieren, in denen auch alles Geschirr gereinigt wird.

Dem Küchenchef unterstehen die Abteilungschefs, der „Saucier", der „Entremetier" (Gemüsekoch), der „Garde=manger" (kalter Koch), der „Rôtisseur" (Bratenkoch), der „Pâtissier" (Süßspeisen=Koch), mit ihren Hilfskräften. Sie bilden eine „Brigade" von 12 Mann. Der Küchenchef entwirft das Menu und gibt den Unterchefs seine Anweisungen betreffs der Zubereitung und der zu verwendenden Mengen. Die Rohmaterialien werden dem neben der Küche gelegenen „Economat" gegen Bons entnommen. Neben diesem Verteilungsraume liegen die Reserve=Vorratsräume. Es sind Kühlräume für Fleisch, Geflügel, Eier, Butter, Konserven, Gemüse. Wie zum Essen das Trinken,

so gehört zur Küche der Keller, der unter der Leitung eines tüchtigen Kellermeisters mit seinen Hilfskräften steht. Ein großes Hotel unterhält Weinlager, in denen enorme Kapitalien angelegt sind. — Die fertigen Speisen wandern vom Herd auf den danebenstehenden Wärmetisch, der in seinem Innern eine Vorrichtung zum Wärmen der Platten birgt. Hier werden sie den Kellnern gegen Bons übergeben. Der „Annonceur", auch „Aboyeur" genannt, schreibt die Bestellungen an eine Tafel und ruft nun nacheinander die fällige Lieferung der fertigen Speisen aus, die von Kellnern in Empfang genommen und eine Treppe hinauf direkt in den Speisesaal getragen werden. — Kehren wir aus der Unterwelt an die Ober-

fläche zurück. An der Spitze des Betriebes steht der Direktor. Der geschäftlichen Verwaltung dienen Rezeption, Kasse, Buchhalterei und Kontrolle. Ein wichtiger Bestandteil der Organisation eines Hotels ersten Ranges ist die Telefonzentrale. Alle Bestellungen im Hause gehen über diese Zentrale. In der Halle ist das uniformierte Personal tätig, der Concierge, der Nacht=Concierge, die Liftiers, die Garderobiers, die Chasseurs für den Hotel= und Stadtdienst, die Konducteurs für den Bahndienst. Das Kellner=Personal besteht aus dem Oberkellner, den Abteilungskellnern mit ihren „Commis", den Zimmerkellnern, den Bar= und Halle=Kellnern, den Kurier=Kellnern für die Bedienung der fremden Dienerschaft. Das Personal auf den Etagen umfaßt die Etagenportiers und Unterportiers, sowie die Zimmermädchen und Hilfszimmermädchen, unter der Aufsicht der „Etagen=Gouvernante". Schließlich ist noch das technische Personal, Heizer, Elektriker, Mechaniker, Schreiner, Maler, Tapezierer und die Wäscherei zu erwähnen. So sieht es hinter den Kulissen jenes Organismus aus, den die Neuzeit aus dem primitiven Gasthof geschaffen hat.

(Die Bilder wurden von unsern Spezialphotographen H. Stauber im Hotel Bellevue Palace und Bernerhof in Bern aufgenommen.)

Hauptküche. „Brigade" an der Vormittagsarbeit.

Blick von der „Kalten Küche", der sogen. Garde=manger, nach der Hauptküche.

Seiten möglich waren, in diese Kategorie. Es gab Geschäftsleute, Verbannte, geheimnisvoll schweigende Herren mit verborgenen Absichten. Es gab exotisch aussehende, elegant angezogene Frauen, die allein sassen und eine streng korrekte Würde an den Tag legten. Zu diesen Dauergästen im Hotel kamen schwer zu beschreibende Individuen, die irgendwelche Aufträge hatten, oder die in den Diensten der Gäste standen.»[8]

Um 1920 begegnen wir im «Bellevue Palace» einem besonderen Gast, dem grossen Lyriker, Schriftsteller, Intellektuellen und Dandy Rainer Maria Rilke. Er war im Juni 1919 von München aus in die Schweiz eingereist und blieb hier bis zu seinem Tod 1926. Wiederholt besuchte er Bern und logierte hier jeweils in seinem «Lieblingshotel». Zwei Tage nach seiner Ankunft im Hotel Bellevue Palace, wo er vom 25. Juni bis zum 9. Juli 1919 wohnte, schrieb Rilke, vom Charme der Zähringerstadt eingenommen, an die Kabarettistin Albertina Cassani: «... dieses schöne Bern, in dem ich erst begreife, was ein ausgeglichenes bürgerliches Wesen in gewissen Zeiten redlich aus sich hervorzubringen vermocht hat: alle diese alten Häuser sind Garantien des guten Willens in jedem Einzelnen und, wie sie aneinander angeschlossen dastehen, ein Beweis gemeinsamen Wollens und Einverstehens». Vom 17. bis zum 19. November gleichen Jahres kam Rilke auf Einladung der Freistudentenschaft für eine Dichterlesung im Grossratssaal nach Bern und traf sich mit befreundeten Bekannten der vornehmeren Berner Gesellschaft zu «Salongesprächen», u.a. mit Yvonne de Wattenwyl, Beatrix von Steiger-von Mülinen, Jean-Jacques von Bonstetten u.a. Und in einem Brief an Nanny

his arrival in Berne, where he stayed from 25th June until 9th July 1919. Rilke described the charming city to soprano Albertina Cassani in these terms: *... this beautiful Berne, where I only now comprehend what a steady bourgeois nature has honourably brought forth in certain times: all these old houses are guarantors of goodwill in each individual and, as they stand next to each other, are proof of communal intent and understanding.* Following an invitation by the Bernese *Freistudentenschaft* [unincorporated students] to read his poetry at the *Grossratssaal*, the great chamber of the Bernese cantonal parliament, Rilke again spent time in the city from 17th until 19th November of the same year. On that occasion he also met with members of Berne's salon society, among them Yvonne de Wattenwyl, Beatrix von Steiger-von Mülinen and Jean-Jacques von Bonstetten. In a letter to Nanny Wunderly-Volkart dated 25th August 1920, written on Bellevue Palace stationery, the poet praised the Bellevue Hotel as the most agreeable such establishement in Switzerland. He further expressed his fascination with the collection of Berne's Historical Museum. In 1923 he was particularly moved by Henri Moser's Cashmere collection: *This time, however, I made an especially interesting discovery: shawls: Cashmere shawls from Persia and Turkistan showed off to their most moving advantage on the gently sloping shoulders of our great-grand-mothers; shawls with a circular or square or star-shaped centre-piece on black, green or ivory ground; each a world unto its own, each in truth a complete happiness, a complete delight, and perhaps a complete renunciation ... as years ago the nature of lace, so, facing these outspread and variegated weavings,*

53 Publireportage in der Schweizer Illustrierten Zeitung, Nr. 22, 1925. – Publicity feature in the *Schweizer Illustrierte Zeitung*, no. 22, 1925.

Wunderly-Volkart vom 25. August 1920, geschrieben auf einem Briefbogen des Bellevue Palace, rühmte der Dichter das «Bellevue» als das für ihn angenehmste Schweizer Hotel und zeigte sich fasziniert von der Sammlung des Historischen Museums in Bern. Besonders nachhaltig berührt hat ihn 1923 die Kaschmir-Sammlung von Henri Moser im Historischen Museum: «Diesmal aber kam ich auf eine besondere Entdeckung: Shawls: persische und turkestanische Kaschmir Shawls, wie sie auf den sanft abfallenden Schultern unserer Ur-Grossmütter zu rührender Geltung kamen; Shawls mit runder oder quadratischer oder sternig ausgesparter Mitte, mit schwarzem, grünem, oder elfenbein-weissem Grund, jeder eine Welt für sich, ja wahrhaftig, jeder ein ganzes Glück, eine ganze Seligkeit und vielleicht ein ganzer Verzicht ... wie vor Jahren die Spitz, so begriff ich plötzlich, vor diesen ausgebreiteten und abgewandelten Geweben, das Wesen des Shawls!» (Brief an die Gräfin Sizzo vom 16. Dezember 1923).⁹ Wohl noch im Hotelzimmer des Bellevue entstanden die ersten Entwürfe zu den wunderbaren Shawl-Gedichten: «O Flucht aus uns und Zu-Flucht in den Shawl ...», «Wie, für die Jungfrau, dem, der vor ihr kniet, die Namen zustürzen unerhört ...» und «Wie Seligkeit in diesem sich verbirgt, ...».

Eher als Kuriosität erhalten blieben Rilkes «Bestellungen» beim «Bellevue Palace»-Coiffeur Schoenauer, ihm einen Flacon des Aftershaves «Arkana» (Kampfer=Toiletten=Wasser), Hautcrème, Gillette-Rasierklingen und einen blutstillenden Stift nachzusenden, die er u.a. während seines Aufenthalts im Palazzo Salis im bündnerischen Solio nicht bekommen konnte. Datiert 2. August 1919 bzw. 26. März 1920.

I suddenly understood the nature of the shawl! (Letter to Margot, Countess Sizzo, dated 16th December 1923).⁹ He most likely penned in his Bellevue hotel room the earliest drafts of his marvellous shawl poems, *O Flucht aus uns und Zu-Flucht in den Shawl ...* (Oh, flight from us and flight into the shawl ...)¹⁰, *Wie, für die Jungfrau, dem, der vor ihr kniet, die Namen zustürzen unerhört ...* (As, of the virgin, of him, who kneels before her, the mind tumbles with tremendous names ...) and *Wie Seligkeit in diesem sich verbirgt, ...* (As bliss concealed in it lies).¹¹

It may be more of a curiosity to see Rilke's requests placed with Schoenauer, the Bellevue Palace barber, for the consignment of a flacon of *Arkana* after-shave (camphor= toilet=water), skin cream, *Gillette* razor blades and a styptic pencil to Palazzo Salis at Solio in the Grisons, where such things were not available (dated of 2nd August 1919 and 26th March 1920, respectively).

The difficult war and post-war years did not fail to affect Berne's hotel trade. When the neighbouring Bernerhof Hotel, which in 1912 had been the venue of a sumptuous state reception for German emperor William II, closed its doors due to economic pressures, the Bellevue Hotel owners acquired the Bernerhof in 1924, adopting the name of *hotel Bellevue Palace und Bernerhof AG* for the successor company. There is no doubt that the Bellevue Palace was intended to tap into the international reputation of the previously illustrious neighbour, whose well-heeled guests would hopefully continue to visit the city and stay at the Bellevue Palace.

54 Rainer Maria Rilke, Passfoto 1919. – Rainer Maria Rilke's passport photograph, 1919.

55 Gedicht «Wie Seligkeit in diesem sich verbirgt». Ausschnitt aus einem der Schals. – Rilke's shawl poem, *Wie Seligkeit in diesem sich verbirgt* (As bliss concealed in it lies); detail of one of the shawls.

56-57 Rainer Maria Rilke. Brief vom 25. Aug. 1920 an Nanny Wunderly-Volkart und Bestellung bei «Bellevue»-Coiffeur Schoenauer. – Rainer Maria Rilke's letter to Nanny Wunderly-Volkart, dated 25th August, 1920, and orders placed with Mr. Schoenauer, the Bellevue hairdresser.

55

54

Shawl

Wie Seligkeit in diesem sich verbirgt,
so eingewirkt, dass nichts mehr sie zerstöre;
wie blosses Spiel vollkommener Akteure
so unverbraucht ins Dauern eingewirkt.

So eingewirkt in schmiegende Figur
ins leichte Wesen dieser Ziegenwolle,
ganz pures Glück, unbrauchbar von Natur
rein aufgegeben an das wundervolle

Geweb in das das Leben überging.
O wieviel Regung rettet sich ins reine
Bestehn und Überstehn von einem Ding.

56

57

Die Auswirkungen der schwierigen Kriegs- und Nachkriegsjahre blieben auch in der Berner Hotellerie nicht aus. Nachdem das Nachbarhotel Bernerhof aus wirtschaftlichen Gründen geschlossen werden musste, kauften die Eigentümer des Hotels Bellevue 1924 den Namen «Bernerhof» und nannten sich fortan «Hotel Bellevue Palace und Bernerhof AG». Gewiss rechnete man damit, zusätzlich von der internationalen Ausstrahlung des «Bernerhofs» zu profitieren und die gutbetuchten Gäste des einst glanzvollen Hotels, wo 1912 der Staatsempfang des deutschen Kaisers Wilhelm II. mit viel Pomp inszeniert worden war, auch für einen Aufenthalt im «Bellevue Palace» begeistern zu können.

1933 starb Fritz Eggimann, der erste Direktor des neuen «Bellevue Palace». Sein Nachfolger wurde Hermann Schmid, den sich die Hotel Bellevue Palace und Bernerhof AG vom Hotel Baur au Lac in Zürich holte. Er liess 1934/35 die ersten Umbauten vornehmen und betraute damit wiederum Max Hofmann. Neben je drei neuen Bädern pro Etage im Nordtrakt entstand ein Café/Tea Room im ehemaligen Billardzimmer an der Ostterrasse.

1936 wollte sich Max Metz, «Bellevue»-Küchenchef und selber Mitaktionär des Hotels, nach vierzig Dienstjahren pensionieren lassen. Erst nach einigem Hin und Her bewilligte ihm der Verwaltungsrat schliesslich «auf Zusehen hin» eine monatliche Pension von 250 Franken.

Während des Zweiten Weltkriegs blieb das Hotel für alle Gäste geöffnet. Der kalte Winter 1941 und die Restriktionen der Heizmittel veranlassten etliche Berner Familien, sich vorübergehend im warmen «Bellevue Palace» einzuquartieren. Am 30. August 1939 war Korpskommandant Henri

1933 saw the death of Fritz Eggimann, the first manager of the new Bellevue Palace. His successor was Hermann Schmid, who had been recruited by the Bellevue Palace und Bernerhof AG from the Baur au Lac in Zurich. In 1934/35 Schmid initiated the first alterations, commissioning Max Hofmann. In addition to three new bathrooms per floor in the north tract, a café/tea-room was installed in the former Billiards Room on the East Terrace.

In 1936, after forty years of service, Max Metz, hotel chef and shareholder in the hotel, decided to retire. Following much discussion by the board of directors, he was awarded a monthly pension of 250 Swiss francs – «until further notice».

During the Second World War the hotel remained open to all guests. The extremely cold winter of 1941 and scarcity of heating fuel prompted numerous Bernese families to take up temporary residence at the cosy Bellevue Palace. On 30th August 1939, one day prior to the outbreak of the Second World War, army commander Henri Guisan was elected general of the Swiss Army. Like Wille, his predecessor in the Great War, Guisan established his headquarters at Berne's Bellevue Hotel. However, he only stayed for a few days, considering the hotel infrastructure as inadequate for the tasks of the General Staff, and the Bellevue as too exposed a location for the army's general headquarters. He was to be proved right, since Berne, London and Madrid were the hubs of international espionage networks throughout the Second World War. Many of the threads intertwined at the bar and in the salons of Berne's elegant establishment.

58–59 Kofferaufkleber 1920er-Jahre. – 1920s luggage stickers.

Guisan einen Tag vor Ausbruch des Zweiten Weltkriegs zum General der Schweizer Armee gewählt worden und bezog, wie General Wille im Ersten Weltkrieg, seinen Kommandoposten im Hotel Bellevue in Bern. Er blieb aber nur wenige Tage, da ihm die Infrastruktur des Hotels für die Arbeit des Generalstabes nicht geeignet und das «Bellevue» als Armeehauptquartier zu wenig abgeschirmt erschien. Zu Recht, wie sich herausstellen sollte.

Während des Zweiten Weltkriegs war Bern neben Madrid und London ein wichtiger Brennpunkt der international verstrickten Spionagenetze. Und viele der Fäden verschlangen sich in den Salons und in der Bar des noblen Gästehauses. In dieser Zeit wurde die «Bellevue-Bar» weltberühmt. So leitete der US-Militärattaché Barnwell Rhett Legge seit 1939 von Bern aus den US-Militärgeheimdienst gegen Nazideutschland und wurde schliesslich selbst Opfer der Bespitzelung durch seinen Schweizer «Kanzleigehilfen» Jakob Fürst. Ab 1942 war der hochkarätigste US-Geheimdienststratege Allen Dulles, der legendäre «Meisterspion von Bern», in der Bundestadt stationiert. Die meisten der berühmten Agentinnen und Spione, unter ihnen die britische Agentin Elizabeth Wiskemann, der Deutsche Hans Bernd Gisevius und andere, gingen im Hotel Bellevue Palace ein und aus. In der «Bellevue-Bar» traf man sich, Diplomaten, Parlamentarier, Botschafter und Militärattachés. Für die Spione und Doppelagenten war die Bar eine ergiebige Informationsquelle und Informationsdrehscheibe. Mitunter wurde selbst das Barpersonal in die Intrigen und Aktionen der Spione verwickelt und immer wieder sorgten Vermutungen über geheime Abhöranlagen im Hotel für Aufregung. Hart-

It was in this period that the Bellevue Bar became world famous. From 1939 the U.S. military attaché, Barnwell Rhett Legge, for example, used Berne as a base to direct military secret service operations against Nazi Germany, eventually falling victim to a spy in his own employ, Swiss clerical assistant Jakob Fürst. From 1942 Allen Dulles was stationed in the Swiss capital. The Swiss Director of the U.S. Office of Strategic Services was dubbed «spy master of Berne». The bar at the Bellevue Palace was the haunt of a number of secret service agents, including Britain's Elizabeth Wiskemann and Germany's Hans Bernd Gisevius, who would gather there to trade information. Of course, diplomats, members of parliament, ambassadors and military attachés also met at the Bellevue Bar. Even bar staff occasionally became involved in the spies' cabals and intrigues; rumours of eavesdropping devices hidden about the hotel repeatedly caused a stir. And there is a persistent rumour of a secret tunnel said to run between the Bellevue Palace Hotel and the Federal Palace. In a miasma of betrayal, conspiracy and seduction, the myths, history and unique atmosphere of the hotel bar combined to produce a chimera of reality and fiction. The Bernese grand-hotel and the notorious Bellevue Bar feature in numerous crime stories, among them a treatment by John le Carré, himself a former agent in the British Secret Service, whose novels explore the unfathomable depths of the spy world. In 1982 some scenes of part three of *Smiley's People*, le Carré's detective trilogy starring Sir Alec Guinness, were shot on location at the Bellevue Palace Hotel. Last but not least, rumours of conspiracies during the so-called Nights of the Long Knives, which usually

näckig halten sich die Gerüchte um einen geheimen Tunnel zwischen dem Hotel Bellevue Palace und dem Bundeshaus. Im Dunstkreis von Verschwörungen, Verrat und Verführung verflechten sich die einzigartige Atmosphäre und die Geschichte der Hotelbar zwischen Wahrheit und Erfindung zum Mythos. In verschiedenen Werken der Literatur finden sich das Berner Grandhotel und seine berühmtberüchtigte «Bellevue-Bar» als Schauplatz von Kriminalgeschichten. Als Beispiel im Werk des weltbekannten Schriftstellers John le Carré, der, selber ehemaliger Mitarbeiter des britischen Geheimdienstes, in seinen Romanen die menschlichen Abgründe der Spionagewelt in allen ihren Facetten und Tiefen auszuleuchten vermag. «Agent in eigener Sache», der dritte Teil seiner Kriminalromantrilogie Smiley's People, wurde mit Sir Alec Guinness in der Hauptrolle zu Teilen 1982 im Bellevue Palace verfilmt. Die «Verschwörungen» in der sogenannten «Nacht der langen Messer» jeweils unmittelbar vor der Wahl des Schweizer Bundesrates nähren bis heute den Mythos der «Bellevue-Bar».

Am 22. Februar 1944 erteilte die Stadt eine «Kleine Baubewilligung» für den Umbau des neuen Billardzimmers im Untergeschoss der Ostterrasse – also unter der heutigen «Münz» – zu einem Gastlokal, damals «Zur Münz / Café • Restaurant • Confiserie», später Grillroom. Verantwortlicher Architekt war nochmals Max Hofmann.

Nach dem Zweiten Weltkrieg genügte die originale Möblierung des Hotels den neuen Standards offenbar nicht mehr. «Antike» Möbel schmückten nun den repräsentativsten Teil der Hotelzimmer und der Gesellschaftsräume. Die «Funk»-Kommoden, die hochlehnigen Barocksessel und

precede the Swiss united parliament's elections to the *Bundesrat*, Switzerland's governing council, continue to keep alive the mythos of the Bellevue Bar.

On 22nd February 1944 the Berne authorities granted a lesser building permit for the conversion of the new billiards rooms in the basement of the east terrace – i.e. underneath today's Münz – into a restaurant, at the time named Zur Münz / Café • Restaurant • Confiserie, later Grill Room. The architect chosen was again Max Hofmann. After the Second World War the hotel's original furnishings were no longer up to the required standard. «Antique» furniture now embellished the most prestigious guest and public rooms. The chests-of-drawers in the style of Funk, the high-backed baroque armchairs and the Rococo furniture were supplied by Switzerland's best furniture and decorating firms. Between 1960 and 1965, the hotel's own cabinet maker produced numerous side tables. Small oil paintings with genre and landscape motifs, no doubt partly from the old Bellevue, made way for reproductions of famous paintings in lavish gilded frames. Between 1938 and 1942 the Bernese painter Dora Lauterburg, and another painter with the initials SH, supplied dozens of floral still-lifes. Oriental carpets now covered not only the parquet floors in the public rooms on the ground floor but also the guest rooms upstairs. The upper corridors were furnished with rustic pieces. In 1957 interior architect F. Bussinger, Berne, oversaw the installation of a new hairdressing salon in the basement. In autumn 1970, under the aegis of Bernese architects, Wander and Leimer, four bathrooms were added on each of the first to fourth floors and the guest rooms renovated.

65

64

61

62

63

60

60–65 Die «Bellevue-Bar» war im Zweiten Weltkrieg für Diplomaten und Agenten eine der wichtigsten Informationsdrehscheiben und weltberühmt. Im Auftrag des US-Geheimdienstes arbeitete damals Allen Dulles (61) in Bern. Das «Bellevue Palace» ist auch Schauplatz etlicher Spionagegeschichten in Literatur und Film. Aufnahme 1963. John le Carré (62) und Sir Alec Guinness (63). – During the Second World War, the Bellevue Bar achieved some notoriety as one of the most important information hubs for diplomats and secret service agents, including Allen Dulles (61), who was working for the U.S. Secret Service. The Bellevue Palace is also the location of various literary and film spy thrillers. Photograph 1963. John le Carré (62) and Sir Alec Guinness (63).

66

67

68

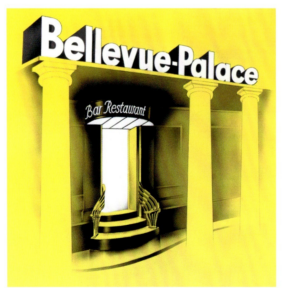
70

71

die Rokoko-Ameublements stammten aus den besten Einrichtungshäusern der Schweiz. Der Hotelschreiner stellte zwischen 1960 und 1965 zahllose Abstelltischchen mit Einlegearbeiten her. Die meist kleinformatigen Ölbilder mit Genre- und Landschaftsmotiven, die zum Teil wohl noch aus dem alten Bellevue stammten, wichen nun Kunstreproduktionen bekannter Gemälde in reichen Goldrahmen. Die Berner Malerin Dora Lauterburg und ein Maler oder eine Malerin «SH» lieferten zwischen 1938 und 1942 Dutzende Blumenstillleben. Orientteppiche nun nicht mehr nur die Gesellschaftsräume im Erdgeschoss, sondern auch die Gästezimmer auf den Etagen. Die Korridore stattete man mit Bauernmöbeln aus. 1957 wurde im Untergeschoss ein neuer Coiffeursalon eingerichtet. Innenarchitekt F. Bussinger, Bern. Im Herbst 1970 wurden durch die Berner Architekten Wander und Leimer im ersten bis vierten Obergeschoss je vier Bäder eingebaut und gleichzeitig die Zimmer renoviert.

Auf Wunsch des Bundesrates erwarb die Schweizerische Nationalbank (SNB) 1976 die Aktienmehrheit des Hotels, das sich in einer kritischen finanziellen Lage befand und in ausländische Hände zu fallen drohte und ermöglichte mit finanziellen Investitionen das Fortbestehen des Hotels.

Sollte innerhalb von zehn Jahren keine andere Trägerschaft gefunden werden, war der Bundesrat bereit, der Bundesversammlung die Rücknahme der Aktien zum tatsächlichen Kaufpreis zu beantragen.[10] Der dringenden Modernisierung des Bellevue Palace stand somit nichts mehr im Weg: Das ehemalige Billardzimmer sollte abgebrochen und die anschliessende Ostterrasse mit dem «Stadtrestaurant zur Münz» überbaut werden. Die entsprechende Bau-

Upon request of the *Bundesrat*, i.e. the Swiss government, the Swiss National Bank (SNB) acquired the majority of the hotel shares in 1976 when the mother company found itself in dire financial straits and foreign interests were baying at the doors. The federal investment ensured the continued existence of the grand-hotel. In the event that a more suitable buyer could not be found within the next ten years, the agreement was for the Swiss government to submit a proposal to the united federal parliaments to buy back the shares at the actual purchase price.[12]

This removed any further obstacles to the urgent upgrading and refurbishment of the Bellevue Palace Hotel: the former Billiards Room was to be demolished and the adjacent East Terrace converted into the City Restaurant Zur Münz. However, the owner of the Mocambo cabaret and dance-hall lodged an appeal claiming that a required exceptional permit had not been obtained. Aimed at thwarting his rivals project, the appeal delayed the required building permit until 8th March 1978. Building work began on 3rd October 1978, and was completed on 26th April 1979. The architects in charge were Schwaar and Schwaar in Berne, with their employees P. Elnegaard and Benedikt Loderer.

Another building permit, of 16th April 1980, allowed the conversion of staff rooms on the attic floor into guest rooms and raising the lift to the fifth floor. Again Schwaar and Schwaar architects were commissioned, this time with their employee H. Ritter.

The lesser building permit of 26th April 1982 foresaw «conversion and renovation», including the «conversion and renovation of existing guest rooms on floors 1–4». Again

66–71 Kinowerbung in den 1950er-Jahren. – 1950s cinema advertisements.

bewilligung verzögerte sich jedoch wegen einer Einsprache bis zum 8. März 1978. Die Bauarbeiten dauerten vom Oktober 1978 bis zum April 1979. Das Projekt lag in den Händen der Architekten Schwaar und Schwaar in Bern, Eine Baubewilligung vom 16. April 1980 erlaubte den Umbau der Personalzimmer im Dachgeschoss zu Gästezimmern und die Weiterführung der Lifte ins fünfte Obergeschoss. Die «Kleine Baubewilligung» vom 26. April 1982 sah «Umbau und Renovation» vor. Sie umfasste den «Umbau und [die] Renovation bestehender Gästezimmer in den Etagen 1–4». Für beide Umbauprojekte zeichneten wiederum die Architekten Schwaar und Schwaar verantwortlich. Als Vorsitzender des Bauausschusses der Hotel Bellevue Palace und Bernerhof AG wirkte Prof. Jean-Werner Huber, der damalige Direktor des Amtes für Bundesbauten (AFB).

Anlässlich des 75-Jahr-Jubiläums der SNB hatte der Bankrat 1982 beschlossen, der Eidgenossenschaft die Bellevue-Aktien als Geschenk anzubieten. Die Annahme dieses Geschenks gestaltete sich allerdings etwas schwierig, da sich das Bellevue Palace damals in einer Renovierungs- und Umstrukturierungsphase befand. 1986 stellten der Bund und die Schweizerische Nationalbank dafür je 20 Millionen Franken bereit. 1991 waren die Bauarbeiten abgeschlossen, und 1994 wurden die Aktien der SNB (99.7% Kapitalanteil) als Geschenk der Eidgenossenschaft übertragen.[11] Von da an präsidierte der Direktor der Eidgenössischen Finanzverwaltung den Verwaltungsrat der AG. Der Verwaltungsrat beschloss, die Gästegeschosse des Hotels restaurieren zu lassen und das Angebot wieder auf den Stand zu heben, den man vom «ersten Haus am Platz» erwartete. Den Auftrag

Schwaar and Schwaar were commissioned with H. Ritter, their construction foreman. Prof. Jean-Werner Huber, then Director of the Office of Federal Buildings (AFB), was appointed chairman of the Building Committee of the Hotel Bellevue Palace und Bernerhof AG.

On the occasion of the 75th anniversary of the Swiss National Bank (SNB) in 1982, the Bank Council decided to offer the Bellevue shares as a gift to the Swiss Confederation. Accepting the gift, however, proved somewhat difficult because the hotel was undergoing major restructuring and refurbishment work, for which, in 1986, the Swiss government and the SNB each provided 20 million Swiss francs. Work was completed in 1991 and in 1994 the SNB's gift of its 99.7% share in the capital was at last transferred to the Swiss Confederation.[13] That was when the director of the Federal Finance Administration (FFA) became President of the Board of Directors of Hotel Bellevue Palace und Bernerhof AG. The board decided to refurbish the guest floors of the hotel in order to raise the standard of the rooms to the level expected of Berne's top hotel. In 2001 architectural firm Jordi und Partner AG were commissioned to design the project, while architect Pia M. Schmid was in charge of the interior design. Estate agents/builders von Graffenried AG Liegenschaften were responsible for the execution of construction work. Melchior Windlin, Bellevue director, and Danilo Menegotto of the Federal Office of Construction and Logistics were joint project leaders. During this major overhaul the hotel proper was closed from January until December 2002; a limited restaurant business was kept going. On New Year's Eve 2002 the hotel reopened its doors to

72

73

74

75

76

77

78

79

80

72–79 Die «Bellevue»-Direktoren / The Bellevue directors: Fritz Eggimann 1913–1933, Hermann Schmid 1933–1949, Jost Schmid 1955–1977, Fritz Mäder 1977–1982, Jacques Künzli 1982–1986, Melchior Windlin 1986–2006, Robert Näpflin 2006/07, Urs Bührer ab 2007.

80 «Schlüsselübergabe» durch Nationalbankpräsident Markus Lusser (links) an Bundespräsident Otto Stich anlässlich der Schenkung der Bellevue-Aktienanteile der Schweizerischen Nationalbank an die Eidgenossenschaft, 1994 – Ceremonial exchange of keys by the President of the Swiss National Bank, Markus Lusser (left), to President of the Federal Council, Otto Stich, on the occasion of the celebration the gift by the Swiss National Bank of Bellevue shares to the Swiss Confederation, 1994.

81 Hotelprospekt aus den 1940er-Jahren. – Hotel brochure from the 1940s.

zur Projektplanung erhielten 2001 die Architekten Jordi und Partner AG, die Innenausstattung betreute die Architektin Pia M. Schmid, die Bauausführung leitete die von Graffenried AG Liegenschaften. Die Projektverantwortung lag in den Händen von Bellevue-Direktor Melchior Windlin und Danilo Menegotto vom Bundesamt für Bauten und Logistik. Für die Umbauarbeiten von Januar bis Dezember 2002 wurde das Hotel geschlossen, der Restaurantbetrieb jedoch in eingeschränktem Umfang weitergeführt. An Silvester konnte der Hotelbetrieb wieder aufgenommen werden. 2005 verkaufte die Hotel Bellevue-Palace AG Grund und Boden des Hotels an die Schweizerische Eidgenossenschaft. 2006 starb Direktor Melchior Windlin. Interimistisch wurde die Leitung Robert Näpflin übertragen. 2007 verpachtete die Hotel Bellevue-Palace AG das Hotel an die Victoria-Jungfrau Collection AG. Zur Hotelgruppe der VJC gehören auch das Victoria-Jungfrau & Spa Interlaken, das Palace Luzern und das Hotel Eden au Lac in Zürich. 2007 übernahm Urs Bührer die Direktion des Hotels. In den folgenden Jahren wurden regelmässig Renovierungs- und Erneuerungsarbeiten durchgeführt: 2008 Renovation der Bellevue Bar. 2009 Aufbau des «BELLEViE-Gym» auf das Dach des Hotels. 2010 Bau und Eröffnung des Fumoirs neben der Bellevue Bar. Umbau der Küche und des gesamten Untergeschosses sowie der technischen Räume. Sanierung der Lüftung in der Lobby sowie die Renovation der Glaskuppel in der Hotelhalle. 2012 Gesamtsanierung der Bellevue-Terrasse, Erneuerung der Präsidentensuiten, 22 Suiten und Süd-Zimmer. Auffrischung des Salon Royal und Einbau modernster Kongresstechnik.

guests. In 2005 Hotel Bellevue-Palace AG sold the property to the Swiss Confederation. Following the death in 2006 of director Melchior Windlin, Robert Näpflin was appointed director ad-interim.

In 2007 Hotel Bellevue-Palace AG leased the hotel to Victoria-Jungfrau Collection AG. The collection also comprises the Victoria-Jungfrau & Spa Interlaken, the Palace Hotel in Lucerne and Hotel Eden au Lac in Zürich. In 2007 Urs Bührer was appointed director of the Bellevue Palace Hotel. In subsequent years renovation and refurbishment work was carried out on a regular basis, including the renovation of the Bellevue Bar in 2008; a rooftop extension in 2009 for the «BELLEViE Gym»; the inauguration in 2010 of a newly installed smoking room next to the Bellevue Bar; the complete refurbishment of the kitchens, basement floor and domestic engineering facilities; upgrading of the lobby ventilation, and restoration of the stained-glass skylight above the foyer. 2012 saw the complete overhaul of the Bellevue Terrasse, the renovation of the Presidential Suite, 22 further suites and south-facing rooms; a «face-lift» for the Salon Royal and the installation of state-of-the-art conference and congress technology.

82 Hotel-Réception. Aktuelle Aufnahme. – Hotel Reception. Recent photograph.

Vom Glanz des Bellevue Palace – Ein Spaziergang durch die Räumlichkeiten
A Tour of the Glorious Bellevue Palace

Das heutige «Bellevue» erstrahlt noch immer im Geist der Tradition des «alten» in seinem ursprünglichen Glanz. Über die Jahrzehnte hinweg blieb der Charme der Gesellschaftsräume, ein grosser Teil der originalen Möblierung und in den Räumlichkeiten viele seiner alten Gemälde erhalten.

Eingangshalle und Palmengarten
Die Atmosphäre der beiden Räume ist geprägt vom gläsernen Zelt über der Hotelhalle, dem «Palmengarten», und der ausladenden Treppe, die links in die erste Etage hinauf führt. Beide stammen aus der Bauzeit. Die ornamentalen Glasmalereien der Hofüberdachung fertigte das Atelier Walther und Müller in Bern an. Die ionischen Säulen des Palmengartens waren ursprünglich steinsichtig. Sie sind seit der Neueinrichtung der Halle 1987 leider mit einem glänzenden Anstrich überzogen.

Salon d'Honneur und La Terrasse
Die beiden Speiseräume gruppieren sich um das zentrale Office herum, so dass alle Säle – häufig gleichzeitig mit ganz verschiedenen Gästegruppen belegt– von dort aus bedient werden können.

In a spirit of tradition, the Bellevue continues to reflect its predecessor's original splendour and the charm of the old salons and parlours. A large portion of the original furnishings and numerous old paintings have been preserved across the decades.

The Hotel Lobby and the Palm Garden
The two spaces go back to the period of construction and are characterised by the stained-glass skylight above the foyer, the Palm Garden and the sweeping staircase leading to the first floor. The glass art was executed by the studio of Walther and Müller in Berne. Regrettably, when the lobby was refurbished in 1987, the Ionic stone columns in the Palm Garden were covered with a coat of varnish.

The dining-rooms: Salon d'Honneur and La Terrasse
All the dining-rooms are grouped around the central plating station to serve several completely different groups of guests.

83 Die Hotelhalle («Palmengarten») heute. - The great hotel lobby (Palm Garden) today.

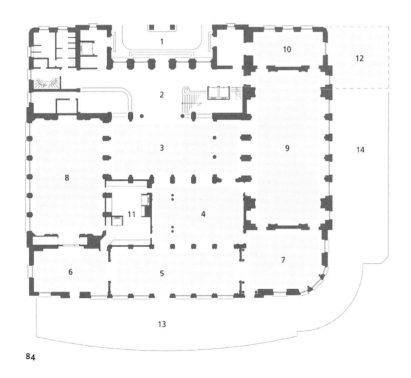

84

85

1 Vorfahrt – Entrance
2 Eingangshalle mit Rezeption und Haupttreppe – Hotel lobby with Reception and main staircase
3 Palmengarten – Palm Garden
4 Salon d'Honneur
5 Restaurant La Terrasse
6 Salon Casino
7 Salon Rouge
8 Salon du Palais
9 Salon Royal
10 Bar
11 Office – Plating station
12 Ehemaliger Billardsaal – Former billiards room
13 Bellevue-Terrasse – Bellevue terrace
14 Zur Münz

84 Hotelgrundriss mit eingetragenen Ziffern zur Raumorientierung. – Floor plan of the Bellevue Palace Hotel with numbers to aid spatial orientation.

85 Salon d'Honneur. Das Wandbild mit einer griechischen Gesellschaftsszene im Salon d'Honneur stammt wahrscheinlich von Otto Haberer-Sinner. – Salon d'Honneur. The mural, probably by Otto Haberer, depicts a Greek group scene.

Der heutige Salon d'Honneur war wohl als «Winterrestaurant» gedacht, für die Jahreszeit also, in der die grossartige Aussicht aus den Fenstern der Südfront weniger vermisst wird. Der Durchgang vom Palmengarten zum Restaurant La Terrasse ist seitlich mit einer Kolonnade vom Salon d'Honneur leicht abgetrennt. Der Raum wirkt als Steigerung des Palmengartens: Nicht mehr ionische Säulen mit Sandsteinschäften, sondern korinthische Marmorsäulen mit patiniert vergoldeten Basen und Kapitellen zieren hier den Saal. Er wird beherrscht vom grossen Kristallüster aus der Bauzeit. Die Schmalseiten des Raums schmücken Spiegel und das Gemälde einer griechischen Gesellschaftsszene, das an Malereien Anselm Feuerbachs erinnert. Das Wandbild stammt wahrscheinlich aus dem Atelier von Otto Haberer, das auch die andern Dekorationsmalereien im Haus geliefert hat.

Nach den reichen Stuckverzierungen und den Vergoldungen der Salons nimmt das raumhoch vertäferte Restaurant La Terrasse mit weissem Gipsgewölbe die Feierlichkeit wieder etwas zurück. Der lichtdurchflutete Speisesaal präsentiert sich als geglückte Mischung aus «Galerie des glaces», der Spiegelgalerie des Sonnenkönigs im Schloss von Versailles und der gediegenen Atmosphäre eines Herrenzimmers. Das Restaurant mit insgesamt nur sechs (statt sieben) Fensterachsen konnte lediglich der Länge nach symmetrisch gestaltet werden, weil der Saal nicht die volle Mitte der Südfront einnimmt, damit auch der kleine Speisesaal (Salon Casino) mit einen schmalen Durchgang mit dem Office verbunden werden konnte. Obwohl heute zwei grosse Deckenleuchter die ursprüngliche Beleuchtung mit

Most likely, today's Salon d'Honneur was conceived as a winter restaurant, i.e. for a season when the magnificent view from the south-facing windows would be less missed. A lateral colonnade provides a subtle division to the passage from the Palm Garden to La Terrasse restaurant. The salon was planned as a further enhancement of the Palm Garden, Ionic columns with sandstone shafts making way for Corinthian marble pillars with patinated gilded bases and capitals. The salon is dominated by large crystal chandeliers from the construction period. The narrow walls of the room are decorated with mirrors and the mural, reminiscent of Anselm Feuerbach's work, of a social gathering *à la grècque*. Now concealed by a baroque Gobelin tapestry, probably originates from the studio of Otto Haberer, which also supplied other decorative artwork in the house.

After the lavish stucco and gilding of the salon, La Terrasse is rather less sumptuous, with panelling to the architraves and white plaster vaulting. The room is a successful combination of Versailles-inspired Hall of Mirrors and smoking room. Because it is not situated in the middle of the south façade, only the long sides of the room are symmetrically subdivided. La Terrasse has six window axes to allow for a connection between the small dining-room and the plating station. Although two large chandeliers have now replaced the original alabaster bowl lights in the lunettes above the windows, the room still breathes a cosy plushness, echoing the guests' anticipation of imminent culinary pleasures.

87

86

86–88 Salon d'Honneur. Aufnahmen aus der Bauzeit, um 1980 und heute. Das Wandbild war zwischen ca. 1980 und 2010 durch einen Gobelin verdeckt. – Salon d'Honneur. Photographs dating from ca. 1913, from ca. 1980 and today. From 1980 until 2010 the mural was concealed by a Gobelin tapestry.

89

93

90

89–91 Restaurant La Terrasse. Aufnahmen aus der Bauzeit, 1938 und heute. – La Terrasse Restaurant. Photographs dating from the time of construction, from 1938 and today.

92–94 Die Bellevue-Terrasse. Aufnahmen 1938, 1950er- und 1960er-Jahre. – The Bellevue Terrace. Photographs dating from 1938, the 1950s and 1960s.

92

94

95

96

97

98

99

95–102 Die «Bellevue-Küche» ist seit den Anfängen des Hotels für ihre kulinarischen Köstlichkeiten berühmt. – Since the beginnings of the hotel, the Bellevue Palace kitchen has been renowned for its culinary delights. – Küchenbrigade 1934 und 2010. – The kitchen staff in 1934 and 2010.

103–109 Die «Bellevue»-Küchenchefs: Max Metz 1895–1936, Cesar Scherrer ab 1936, P. Rüegsegger ab ca. 1947, Gottfried (Godi) Burkhard ab 1960, Roland Jöhri 1978–1983, Heinrich Lauber 1983–2006, Gregor Zimmermann ab 2007. – The Bellevue chefs: Max Metz, 1895–1936, Cesar Scherrer, from 1936, P. Rüegsegger, from ca. 1947, Gottfried (Godi) Burkhard, from 1960, Roland Jöhri, 1978–1983, Heinrich Lauber, 1983–2006, Gregor Zimmermann, since 2007.

103

104

105

106

107

108

109

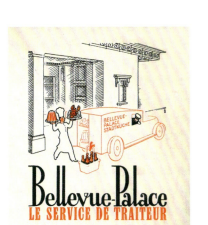
100

101

102

Alabasterschalen in den Stichkappen über den Fenstern und den rückseitigen Spiegeln ersetzt haben, strahlt der Raum immer noch festliche Behaglichkeit aus – Vorfreude auf den kulinarischen Genuss.

Salon Casino (kleiner Speisesaal) und Salon Rouge

Die beiden Ecksäle erfüllten früher ganz verschiedene Aufgaben. Heute dient der Salon Casino als Speisesaal für private Gesellschaften, kann bei grossen Banketten aber auch als Erweiterung des grossen Speisesaals (Salon du Palais) verwendet werden. In seiner Ausgestaltung wird das Versailles-Motiv des Restaurants weitergesponnen. Die Anklänge an den «Salon de la Paix» an der Spiegelgalerie in Versailles sind hier zwar verhalten, aber deutlich formuliert. Lange waren die amüsanten Genreszenen aus dem Atelier Haberer-Sinner oberhalb der Vertäfelung überstrichen, wurden aber 1987 neu «entdeckt» und restauriert. Der Holländerleuchter aus der Bauzeit wurde bei der Restaurierung durch einen Kronleuchter aus Murano-Glas ersetzt.

Der Salon Rouge in der prominenteren Ostecke des Hotels bildet im Raumkonzept die stille Zuflucht, ist aber sowohl mit dem Salon d'Honneur als auch mit der ehemaligen Hotelhalle und dem Restaurant La Terrasse verbunden. Er war wohl ursprünglich als Damensalon gedacht, ist heute Ort mittelgrosser Anlässe ganz unterschiedlicher Art. Die weissen Stuckaturen im Empirestil kontrastieren festlich mit den intensiv roten Wandbespannungen und Vorhängen. Der Wandschmuck und der grosse Kristallleuchter betonen die «schwierige» Raumform, die durch das Bogenfenster im Rund des «Mittelrisalits» noch unterstrichen wird.

Salon Casino (small dining-room) and Salon Rouge

In earlier times the two corner rooms were allocated quite different purposes. Today the Salon Casino is used as a dining-room for private functions. In the event of large banquets, however, it can also be used as an extension of the large dining-room (Salon du Palais). The restaurant's Versailles theme is further developed in this room in discreetly yet clearly suggested allusions to the Salon de la Paix adjacent to the Hall of Mirrors at Versailles. For quite some time the light-hearted genre scenes on the panelling, also originating from Haberer's studio, had been painted over; in 1987 they were rediscovered and subsequently restored. On the occasion of that restoration, the ... chandeliers from ca. 1913 were replaced by an enormous Murano glass chandelier. In the architectural concept, the Salon Rouge in the (more prominent) east corner of the hotel forms a quiet refuge; it is, however, linked with the Salon d'Honneur, as well as with the former hotel lobby and La Terrasse restaurant. Probably intended as a ladies' salon, it is today a venue for medium-sized functions of all kinds. The white stucco in Empire style provides a splendid contrast to the intensive red wall coverings and curtains. The wall decorations and large chandelier underline the awkward shape of the room, which, regrettably, is further emphasized by the semi-circular windows in the rounded corners of the central projection.

110

110–112 Salon Casino. Aktuelle Aufnahmen der Friesmalereien von Otto Haberer-Sinner. Der kleine Speisesaal um 1950. – Recent photographs of Otto Haberer-Sinner's frieze paintings. The small dining-room c.1950.

111

112

114

113

115

118

116

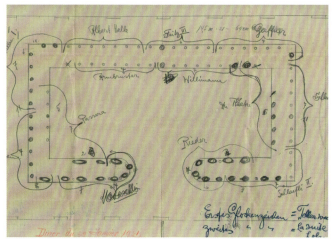
117

113–115 Salon Rouge. Aufnahmen aus der Bauzeit und heute. Vorbereitung eines Festbanketts unter der Leitung von Edi Corpataux, des legendären Grand Maître d'Hôtel von 1952 bis 1987. – Salon Rouge. Photographs dating from the time of construction, and today. Legendary Grand Maître d'Hôtel, Edi Corpataux (1952-1987), is overseeing preparations for a banquet.

116–118 Die Menukarte zum Galadiner vom 29. Januar 1921 und das zugehörige, von Oberkellner Fritz Bourquin (118) gezeichnete Organisationsschema für den Serviceablauf. – Menu of the gala dinner of 29th January, 1921, and the organisational chart drawn up by Fritz Bourquin (118), Maître d'hôtel, to ensure its smooth progression.

119–121 Service Brigade 1934, 60er-Jahre und ca. 2005. – Photographs of Bellevue staff, 1934, the 1960s and ca. 2005.

119

120

121

122

123

124

125

126

127

128

122–129 Der Speise- und Festsaal (Salon du Palais). Aufnahmen aus der Bauzeit, 1938, 1960er-Jahre und heute. 1932 fand im Salon du Palais ein Internationales Fechtturnier der Damen statt. – The Salon du Palais, the Bellevue's grand dining and banqueting hall. Photographs dating from ca. 1913, from 1938, the 1960s and today. During the 1932 Summer Olympics, the Salon du Palais was the venue of the Women's foil tournament.

Salon du Palais (Speisesaal)

Der grosse Speise- und Festsaal mit Fenstern gegen Westen ist mit weissen Stuckaturen im Stil Louis-seize und mit Marmorplatten auf den Pfeilern aus dem selben Stein wie die Säulen im Salon d'Honneur geschmückt. Wahrscheinlich seit dem Anbau des Restaurants Zur Münz auf der Ostseite ist der Deckenspiegel in Altrosa mit glänzender Oberfläche gestrichen. Eine Zeit lang diente der Raum als Ersatz für die Hotelhalle auf der Ostseite, die nach dem Anbau des Restaurants Zur Münz 1978/79 fensterlos wurde und so diese Aufgabe nicht mehr erfüllen konnte. Der rote Deckenanstrich bricht die Feierlichkeit des Saales leicht und macht ihn optisch auch niedriger. Die beiden grossen Lüster und beinahe unzählige Wandappliken können den Raum in ein verschwenderisches Licht tauchen. Der Salon du Palais steht in seiner eleganten Ausgestaltung dem Burgerratssaal im benachbarten Casinobau sehr nahe.

Salon Royal (ehemalige Hotelhalle)

Die ehemalige Hotelhalle mit ursprünglich freiem Blick Richtung Osten und in die Berge ist heute blind. Der Anbau des Stadtrestaurants Zur Münz beraubte sie ihrer Aussicht und des Tageslichts. Das fällt heute, da ohnehin alle Anlässe bei Kunstlicht stattfinden, nicht weiter auf. Der bei weitem grösste Saal des Bellevue war früher durch Pflanzengruppen in lauschige Nischen unterteilt. Zu diesem Konzept gehört das ovale, von reichen Stuckverzierungen umspielte, Gemälde an der Nordwand: Die füllige Lyra-Spielerin hat sich inmitten einer reizenden Zuhörerschar von «Blumenkindern» unter einem Baum niedergelassen. Das Ölgemälde ist mit «Otto Haberer-Sinner, Febr. 1913» signiert.

Salon du Palais (dining-room)

The large dining and banqueting room with windows west-facing is decorated with white stucco in the style of Louis XVI and marble pilasters on the pillars made of the same stone as in the Salon d'Honneur. Probably since the time of the extension of the Restaurant Zur Münz on the east side, the mirrored ceiling has been painted in glossy vieux-rose. For a while the room was used as a replacement of the hotel lobby on the east side, which became windowless on the addition of the Restaurant Zur Münz and was therefore no longer fit for its original purpose. The glossy red ceiling both attenuates the formality of the room and makes it look lower. The two large chandeliers and almost innumerable wallmounted lights can immerse the room in an extravagant light. The Salon du Palais is closely resembles the *Burgerratssaal* in the Casino (also built by Lindt and Hofmann).

Salon Royal (former hotel lobby)

The former hotel lobby originally enjoyed an unimpeded view towards the east and the mountains is now windowless, the addition of the Restaurant Zur Münz having robbed the room of its view and daylight. The lack of daylight is barely noticeable, as artificial lighting is used for all the functions held here. In former times this was by far the largest room in the Bellevue Hotel, and was subdivided into snug niches by group of plants. The oval oil painting on the north wall is part of this concept: in the shade of a tree a Rubenesque lyre player charms three delightful «flower children» at her feet. The painting bears the inscription, «Otto Haberer-Sinner, fec. 1913». Low sofas, comfortable leather armchairs

130 Salon Royal. Bereit für das Festbankett anlässlich des Staatsempfangs des russischen Staatspräsidenten Dmitri Medvedev 2009. – Salon Royal – Ready for the banquet on the state visit of the then President of Russia, Dmitry Anatolyevich Medvedev, in 2009.

131

LEGACION DEL URUGUAY

BERNE, le 25 août MCMXX

DINER
en honneur du Conseil Fédéral Suisse

MENU
CONSOMMÉ BRÉSILIEN
FILETS DE SOLE MARGUÉRY
NOISETTES DE BREBIS
CRÈME DE CHAMPIGNONS
POMMES SOUFFLÉES
CHAUDFROID DE VOLAILLE LUCULLUS
SALADE WALDORF
ASPERGES DU VALAIS
SAUCE MOUSSELINE
VACHERIN BELLEVUE PALACE
JARDINIÈRES DE FRUITS

VILLENEUVE · RICHEBOURG · ROEDERER

132

Chicken Broth
Clear

Chaudfroid de Langouste
Normande

Ris de Veau glacé
Champignons à la Crème

Cailles des Vignes
au Jus d'Ananas
Salade des Primeurs

Briques glacées
Pompadour
Tourte aux Amandes

Paniers
de Fruits

26 Janv. 1921.

134

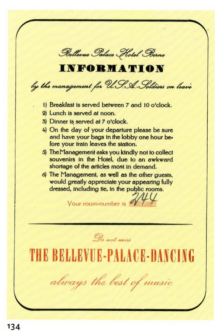

135

133

DINER
offert par

Son Excellence Madame Perón

aux Autorités Helvétiques
et Messieurs les Chefs de Mission Diplomatiques

Berne, le 5 août 1947

VINS

Wodka Russe

Mont d'Or, Goût du Conseil 1943

Château Calon Segur Saint Estèphe 1937

Louis Roederer brut 1928

MENU

Caviar Malossol-Blinis

Homard froid à la Strasbourgeoise
Sauce Coraille
Salade Calipso

Tassette de Térapine Amontillado

Filet de bœuf piqué
Sauce Périgueux
Pommes nouvelles

Petits pois de Nice
aux pointes d'asperges

Pêches flambées à l'Armagnac
Biscuits champagne

131–138 Salon Royal. Die ehemalige grosse Hotelhalle dient bis heute als Speisesaal und Eventlokalität. – Das Ölgemälde der Lyra-Spielerin im Salon Royal von Otto Haberer-Sinner, 1913. – Salon Royal. The former large hotel lobby continues to be used as a dining room and event venue. – The 1913 oil painting by Otto Haberer-Sinner depicting a lyre player, in the Salon Royal.

136

137

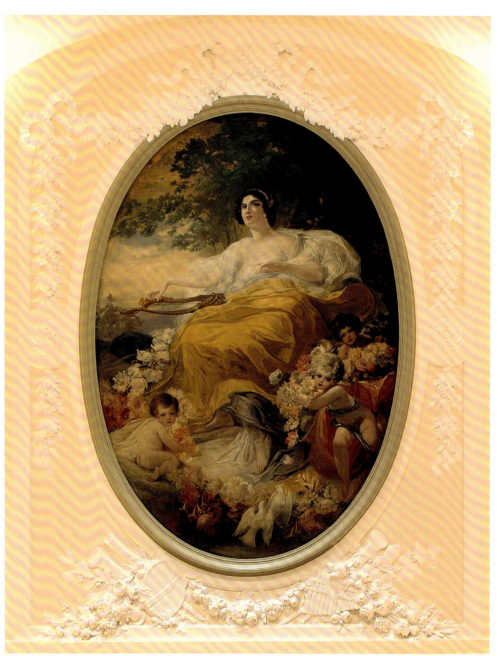
138

Der Lyra-Spielerin zu Füssen standen ehemals tiefe Sofas, bequeme Ledersessel und zierliche Teetische, so dass die unterschiedlichsten Bedürfnisse der vornehmen Gäste im selben Raum befriedigt werden konnten – eine typische Hotelhalle eben. Heute dient die ehemalige Hotelhalle als Auditorium und Bankettsaal. Seine ursprünglichen, eigenartigen, grossen Messingkronleuchter wurden zu unbestimmter Zeit mit Kristallleuchtern vertauscht.

Bar, ehemaliges Billardzimmer, Restaurant Zur Münz und Grillroom

Die heutige Bellevue-Bar diente zuerst als Lese- und Schreibzimmer für die Herren, bildete also das Pendant zum Damensalon (Salon Rouge) auf der gegenüberliegenden Seite der damaligen Hotelhalle. Die Füllungen der Wandtäfer waren mit olivfarbenem Damast bespannt. An diesen Raum schloss sich bis 1944 das Billardzimmer an, das auch eine Bar enthielt. Seine Wände waren mit pompejanischen Malereien geschmückt, die wohl auch aus dem Atelier Haberer stammten. Es wurde bereits 1944 in ein Café umgebaut und nach Süden erweitert. Der Raum muss schon kurz darauf als Grillroom gedient haben. Dieser einzige Anbau am kompakten Baukörper des Hotels fiel 1978/79 dem Stadtrestaurant Zur Münz zum Opfer. Die Idee der Erweiterung des Hotels durch ein Restaurant, das sich an die Kundschaft aus der Stadt richtete, stiess nicht überall auf Zustimmung. Die aus der Fensterfront des dahinter liegenden Salon Royal entwickelte Fassadengestaltung stellt für ihre Bauzeit den erstaunlich gut gelungenen Versuch dar, die Hotelarchitektur mit «modernen» Mitteln fortzusetzen. Das Stadt-

and dainty tea tables were placed below the painting, at the lyre player's feet. As in any hotel lounge, the elegant guests' every need could thus be satisfied in one and the same location. Today the hall is serves as an auditorium and banqueting-hall. At some point in the past, the unique big brass candelabra were replaced by crystal chandeliers.

Bar, former Billiards Room, Restaurant Zur Münz and Grill Room

Originally a reading and writing room, the gentlemen's counterpart to the ladies' salon (Salon Rouge) on the other side of what was then the hotel lobby, today's Bellevue Bar sported panels covered in olive-green damask. Until 1944 it adjoined the Billiards Room, which also contained a bar, and whose walls were decorated with Pompeian paintings, probably also from Haberer's studio. Already in 1944 it was converted into a café and extended towards the south; it may well have been used as a grill room from that time. In 1978/79 the single extension to the compact building unit had to make way for the Restaurant Zur Münz. However, the idea of extending the hotel by adding a restaurant aimed at the city's clientele did not meet with approval from all quarters. In its day, the façade eastward of the Salon Royal windows represented a highly successful attempt to blend the hotel's traditional architecture with a more modern style and structure. Zur Münz opened in spring 1979. In the context of its construction, the Grill Room was relocated to the floor below, and incorporated into the expanded La Terrasse restaurant in 2007. Today the Münz is being used as an event venue in combination with the Salon Royal.

139 Die «Bellevue-Bar» heute. – The Bellevue Bar today.

140

141

142

143

144

145

146

147

140–147 Bar und Billardzimmer im ehemaligen Annexbau im Norden der Ostterrasse. Die heutige Bellevue-Bar war ursprünglich Schreib- und Lesezimmer. Aufnahmen aus der Bauzeit. Die «Bellevue-Bar» um 1938, in den 1980er-Jahren und heute. – Die Baronessen von Senger, gemalt von Anton Einsele, 1859. – Bar and Billiard Room in the former annex to the north of the East Terrace. Today's Bellevue Bar was originally a writing and reading room. Photographs dating back to the construction period. The Bellevue Bar, ca. 1938, in the 1980s and today. – The Baronesses von Senger, painted in 1859 by Anton Einsele, imperial and royal court painter in Vienna.

restaurant Zur Münz wurde im Frühling 1979 eröffnet. Mit dem Bau des Restaurants wurde der Grillroom ins Untergeschoss verlegt und schliesslich 2007 im Zusammenhang mit der Verlegung des Restaurationsbetriebs ins Restaurant La Terrasse geschlossen. Die «Münz» wird heute in Verbindung mit dem Salon Royal als Event-Lokalität genutzt.

Konferenzgeschoss

Im Verlauf der Zeit entstanden im ersten Obergeschoss Sitzungszimmer und Konferenzräume. Aber erst der Umbau des Jahres 2002 schuf dort eine eigentliche Konferenzzone mit der nötigen Infrastruktur. Die Räume nehmen einige der alten Kunstwerke auf, die wahrscheinlich bereits das erste Hotel Bellevue geziert hatten. Zu diesen gehört wohl auch das Porträt dreier junger Damen im Konferenz-Foyer. Das Gemälde trägt auf der Rückseite den Vermerk «Amalia, Johanna und Karoline Baronessen von Senger, gemalt von Anton Einsele, k. k. Hofmaler in Wien, im Jahre 1859, 600 Gulden». Ob wohl Baron von Senger das prächtige Porträt seiner «Drei Töchter» dem alten Bellevue anstelle der Bezahlung überlassen musste, bleibt ein Geheimnis.

The conference floor

Over time, the first floor saw the creation of meeting and conference rooms. Dedicated conference facilities with the necessary infrastructure, however, were only installed during the 2002 renovation. The rooms thus created house some of the old works of art which most likely already adorned the first Bellevue Hotel, among them the painting of three young ladies that can now be admired in the conference foyer. The back of the painting has been inscribed *Amalia, Johanna and Karoline, Baronesses von Senger, painted by Anton Einsele, imperial and royal court painter in Vienna, in the year 1859, 600 Guilders*. Might Baron von Senger have had to relinquish his «Three Daughters» to the old Bellevue in settlement of his hotel bill?

Gästezimmer und Suiten

Die vier ausschliesslich den Hotelgästen vorbehaltenen Obergeschosse wurden 2002 umfassend renoviert. Dabei behielten die Gästezimmer weitgehend ihre originalen Raumhüllen, die Sanitär- und Serviceräume wurden aber erneuert und den Standards eines Fünfsternehotels angepasst. Auf der Beletage stattete man die kleine und die grosse Präsidentensuite aus Sicherheitsgründen mit gepanzerten Türen und schusssicheren Fensterverglasungen aus. Die Gästezimmer und Suiten wurden teilweise mit originalen Möbeln neu eingerichtet und mit Gemälden und Grafiken der im Laufe der Jahre zusammengekommenen Kunstsammlung geschmückt. In den Korridoren richtete man die ehemaligen Ruhezonen in der Südwest- und Südostecke wieder her, so dass sie heute wieder Tageslicht erhalten.

The guest rooms and suites

The four floors exclusively reserved for guests were completely refurbished in 2002. To a large extent, the rooms retained their original shells, but bathrooms (and service spaces) were adapted to the standards of a modern five-star hotel. For security reasons, steel-reinforced doors and bullet-proof window panes were fitted in the large and small Presidential Suites on the *piano nobile*.

Some of the guest rooms and suites were refurbished and original furniture brought back in. Paintings and graphic art from the hotel art collection accumulated across the years are on display in some of the rooms. Quiet zones were reinstated in the hallway areas of the south-west and south-east corners, which again enjoy daylight.

148 Die Präsidentensuite auf der Beletage. – The Presidential Suite on the *piano nobile*.

149

150

153

151

152

149–154 Die Gästezimmer. – Schlafzimmer und Bad. Erste Ausstattung bei der Eröffnung des Hotels 1913. – Salons und Schlafzimmer haben nach dem Zweiten Weltkrieg verschiedene Umbauten erlebt und wurden bis heute jeweils den sich wandelnden Gästewünschen angepasst und erneuert. Preisliste aus den 1940er-Jahren. – Guest bedroom and private bathroom. Original furnishings dating from the opening of the hotel in 1913. – Since the Second World War, the salons and bedrooms have been refurbished on various occasions. Room rates in the 1940s.

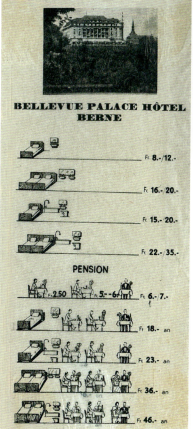

154

155

156

155–156 1957 eröffnete der neue Coiffeur-Salon im Untergeschoss. – A new hairdressing salon was opened in the basement in 1957.

Die Gästebücher
The Visitor's Books

Es scheint paradox. Das Hotel Bellevue Palace lebt in erster Linie für und von der Individualität jedes einzelnen seiner Gäste, und viele gekrönte Häupter und Persönlichkeiten aus Politik und Kultur haben sich in die Gästelisten eingetragen: Königin Nazli von Ägypten, Pablo Casals, Augusto Giacometti, Sir Winston Churchill, GI-General John C. H. Lee, Walt Disney, Juliette Gréco, Sherpa Tenzing, Moshe Dayan, Sophia Loren, Yassir Arafat, John le Carré, Shirley Bassey, Königin Elizabeth II. von England und Prinz Philip, Papst Johannes Paul II., die Musikband Supertramp, Richard von Weizsäcker, Desmond Tutu, Fidel Castro, Li Lanqing, König Hussein I. und Königin Noor von Jordanien, Montserrat Caballé, Prinz Charles, Dmitri Anatoljewitsch Medvedev. Die Aufzählung liesse sich schier endlos weiterführen.

Die Gästebücher und Gästelisten hüten jedoch die Geheimnisse der Persönlichkeiten und Berühmtheiten, die im Berner Luxushotel seit seiner Eröffnung vor einhundert Jahren abgestiegen sind. Akribisch hingekritzelte oder in grosser Geste schwungvoll hingeworfene Unterschriften geben lediglich Namen und Jahreszahlen preis, hier und dort ergänzt durch einen kurzen Eintrag, in den wenigs-

Paradoxical though it may seem, the Bellevue Palace Hotel primarily exists for and through each one of its guests. The names of many a crowned head and other illustrious members of the world's exalted cultural and political circles crop up in the hotel's guest lists. Among them are Queen Elizabeth II of England and Prince Philip, Queen Nazli of Egypt, Sir Winston Churchill, Pablo Casals, Augusto Giacometti, GI General John C. H. Lee, Walt Disney, Juliette Gréco, Sherpa Tenzing, Moshe Dayan, Sophia Loren, Yassir Arafat, John le Carré, Shirley Bassey, Pope John Paul II, The Who, Richard von Weizsäcker, Desmond Tutu, Fidel Castro, Li Lanqing, King Hussein I and Queen Noor of Jordania, Montserrat Caballé, Prince Charles, Dmitri Anatolyevich Medvedev – the list of names could be extended almost into infinity.

The registers and visitor's books, however, keep safe the secrets of all the illustrious guests who have stayed at the Bernese luxury hotel since it opened its doors one-hundred years ago. Their signatures – painstakingly penned or jotted down in gestures of great elan – reveal no more than names and years, occasionally complemented with a brief note, and only very rarely illustrated by a photograph. While some

157 Staatsbesuch 2011: Pratibha Patil, indische Staatspräsidentin, und Bundespräsidentin Micheline Calmy-Rey. – State visit 2011: Pratibha Patil, President of India, and Micheline Calmy-Rey, President of the Swiss Federal Council.

ten Fällen illustriert mit einer Fotografie. Die Geschichten und Anekdoten verblassen langsam in der Erinnerung der Hotelangestellten oder werden zu beeindruckenden Stories zusammengebacken. Andererseits hält die stumme Auflistung der Gästenamen manch erhellende Erkenntnis bereit, deckt da und dort interessante «Zufälligkeiten» auf.

anecdotes and episodes about their guests have faded from the memories of staff members, others have expanded into impressive narratives. On the other hand, the muted lists of names also hold some revealing insights, and may intimate the occasional interesting «coincidence».

S.K.H. Fuad I, König von Ägypten, 1929
S.D. Franz Fürst und Elsa Fürstin von Liechtenstein, 1929
S.K.H. Prinz Heinrich zu Meklenburg, Prinzgemahl von Wilhelmina Königin der Niederlande, 1930
S.K.H. Prinz Carol von Rumänien, 1930
Arturo Toscanini, italienischer Dirigent, 1930
S.K.H. Faisal I., König von Irak, 1930
Herbert von Beneckendorff und Hindenburg, 1930
S. Excl. Emilio Portes Gil, Staatspräsident von Mexiko, 1931
S.K.H. Wilhelmina Helena Pauline Maria von Oranien-Nassau, Königin der Niederlande, 1931
S.K.H. Alfonso XIII., König von Spanien, 1931
María Del Rosario, Herzogin von Alba, 1931
S.K.H. Carl Eduard, Herzog von Sachsen-Coburg und Gotha, 1934
Erzherzog Franz Josef von Österreich, 1935
Prinz David Mdivani, Ehemann von Öl-Erbin Virginia Sinclair, 1936
Paula Wessely-Hörbiger, österreichische Schauspielerin, 1937
Attila Hörbiger, österreichischer Schauspieler, 1937
Paul Muni, US-amerikanischer Schauspieler, 1937
Bruno Walter, deutsch-österreichischer Pianist und Komponist, 1938
Hans Albers, deutscher Schauspieler und Sänger, 1938
Alwine Dollfuss, Witwe des ermordeten österr. Bundeskanzlers, 1938
Eva Curie, Tochter von Marie und Pierre Curie, 1938
General Henri Guisan, Oberbefehlshaber der Schweizer Armee, 1939
Gret Palucca, deutsche Tänzerin, 1940
Maurice Chevalier, französischer Schauspieler und Chansonsänger, 1941
S.K.H. Duarte Herzog von Bragança, Prinz von Portugal, 1941

Franz Léhar, österreichischer Komponist, 1942
N. Nomura, Vize Admiral der japanischen Flotte, 1942
S.Excl. Aziz Izzet Pasha, ägyptischer Regent, 1942
Friedrich Christian Prinz von Schaumburg Lippe, 1942
S.K.H. Juan de Borbón y Battenberg, Conde de Barcelona, 1942
Wilhelm Furtwängler, deutscher Dirigent und Komponsit, 1943
Fürst von Bismark, 1943
S.K.H. Prinz Nicolas, Regent von Rumänien, 1943
Jean Alexandre Steriadi, rumänischer Maler, 1943
S.D. Pierre Prince de Monaco, 1943
S.D. Fürst Franz Josef II. und Gina von Liechtenstein, 1943
Prinzessin Aga Khan, 1943
Sir Dingle Mackintosh Foot, britischer Politiker, 1945
Dr. Lauchlin Bernard Currie kanadischer Economist und angeblicher Sowjet Spion, 1945
Augusto Giacometti, Schweizer Maler, 1945
S. Excl. Sean Lester, letzter Generalsekretär des Völkerbundes, 1946
S.K.H. Félix, Prinz von Luxembourg, 1946
Prinzessin Maria Pia de Bourbon, 1946
General Chang Chen, Generalstabchef der Republik China, 1946
Kurt von Schuschnigg, ehem. österreichischer Bundeskanzler, 1946
Sidney Beer, britischer Kapellmeister, 1946
Louis Kentner, ungarisch-britischer Pianist, 1946
Yehudi Menuhin, Violonist und Dirigent, 1946
S. Excl. Trygve Li, erster Uno Generalsekretär, 1946
S.K.H. Nazli von Ägypten, zweite Frau von König Fuad, 1946
S.K.H. Prinzessin Faikah und Prinzessin Fathaya, 1946
S. Excl. Ramon Serrano Suner, spanischer Aussenminister, 1946

S. Excl. Sir Winston und Mary Churchill, britischer Premierminister, 1946
Giacomo Lauri-Volpi, italienischer Tenor, 1947
S. Excl. Pridi Banomyong, siamesischer Ministerpräsident, 1947
Barbara Hutton und Prinz Igor Trubetzkoy, Erbin von Milliardär Frank W. Woolworth, 1947
Baron Carl Gustaf Emil Mannerheim, finnischer Marschall, 1947
S. Excl. Ferenc Nagy, ungarischer Ministerpräsident, 1947
Thomas Mann, Schriftsteller, 1947
S.K.H. Grossherzogin Charlotte und Félix Prinz von Luxembourg, 1947
S. Excl. Evita Perón, Präsidentin der Republik Argentinien, 1947
General Jean de Lattre de Tassigny, Generalstabchef der französischen Armee, 1947
S. Excl. Paul Henri Spaak, Premierminister des Königreichs Belgien, 1947
Paula Wessely und Attila Hörbiger, österreichisches Schauspielerpaar, 1947
S. Excl. Leopold Figl, Bundeskanzler der Republik Österreich, 1948
S. Excl. Chen Li Fu, Vize Parlamentspräsident der Republik China, 1948
Fredric March, US-Schauspieler und Oskargewinner, 1948
S. Excl. Ganesh Vasudev Mavalankar, Sprecher des Indischen Parlaments, 1948
Arthur Rubinstein, polnischer Pianist, 1948
General Karam Singh, indischer Oberbefehlshaber, 1949
S. Excl. Pandit Jawaharlal Nehru, erster Ministerpräsident der Republik Indien, 1949
Walt Disney, amerikanischer Filmproduzent, 1949
S. Excl. Chaim Weizmann, Statspräsident von Israel, 1949
S.K.H. Akihito, Kronprinz und späterer Kaiser von Japan, 1953

158

161

162

160

159

158–164 Bei Staatsempfängen dinieren und wohnen die Gäste der Eidgenossenschaft im «Bellevue Palace» – The guests at Switzerland's State receptions traditionally reside and dine at the Bellevue Palace Hotel: Manuel Prado y Ugarteche, peruanischer Staatspräsident, mit Bundespräsident Max Petitpierre (1960) – Fürst Rainier III. und Fürstin Gracia von Monaco mit Bundespräsident Max Petitpierre und Gattin (1960) – Königin Elizabeth II. von England (1980) – König Carl XVI. Gustav und Königin Silvia von Schweden, Staatsbankett mit Bundespräsident Kurt Furgler und Vize-Bundespräsident Alphons Egli (1985) – Wen Jibao, chinesischer Ministerpräsident (2009). – Aung San Suu Kyi, burmesische Politikerin (2012).

163

164

Raymond Lambert, Besteiger des Mount Everest, 1953
Sherpa Tenzing Norgay, Besteiger des Mount Everest, 1953
S. Excl. P. Pibulsonggram, Premierminister des Königreichs Thailand, 1955
Charlie Chaplin, Schauspieler und Filmregisseur, 1955
Bruno Walter, deutsch-österreichischer Pianist und Komponist, 1956
S.Excl. Ahmed Soekarno, Staatspräsident der Republik Indonesien, 1956
S.K.H. Dom Duarte Duc de Bragança, portugiesischer Thronfolger, 1956
S. Excl. Julius Raab, Bundeskanzler der Republik Österreich, 1956
S. Excl. William Tubman, Staatspräsident von Liberia, 1956
S. Excl. Theodor Heuss, Staatspräsident der Bundesrepublik Deutschland, 1957
S. Excl. Habib Bourguiba, Staatspräsident der Republik Tunesien, 1957
S. Excl. Adolf Schärf, Bundespräsident der Republik Österreich, 1958
Marc Chagall, französischer Maler, 1958
S.Excl. Pierre Mendès France, ehem. französischer Premierminister, 1958
S.K.H. Paul I und Königin Frédérique von Griechenland, 1958
S. Excl. Manuel Prado y Ugarteche, Staatspräsident der Republik Peru, 1960
S. Excl. Arturo Frondizi, Premierminister der Republik Argentinien, 1960
S.K.H. Bhumibol Adulyadej und Königin Sirikit von Thailand, 1960
S.D. Prinz Rainer III. und Fürstin Grace von Monaco, 1960
S. Excl. Franz Heinrich Lübke, Staatspräsident der Bundesrepublik Deutschland, 1961
Rafael Kubelik, Schweizer Dirigent, 1962
S. Excl. Dr. Alfons Gorbach, Bundeskanzler der Republik Österreich, 1962
S. Excl. Giovanni Gronchi, Staatspräsident der Republik Italien, 1962
S.K.H. Umberto II., Exkönig von Italien, 1962
S.K.H. Prinz Bernhard, Prinzgemahl von Juliana Königin der Niederlande, 1962
S. Excl. Sithu U Thant, Uno Generalsekretär, 1962
S.K.H. Mwambusta IV Bangiricenge, König von Burundi, 1962
S. Excl. Per Christian Haekkerup, Aussenminister des Königreichs Dänemark, 1963
Luitpold Herzog von Bayern, 1964

S.K.H. Frederik IX. und Königin Ingrid von Dänemark, 1965
S.K.H. Prinz Hatachi Masahito, Jüngerer Bruder von Kaiser Akihito von Japan, 1965
S. Excl. Gerhard Schröder, Aussenminister und späterer deutscher Bundeskanzler, 1966
S.K.H. Albert de Liege, Prinz von Belgien und späterer König Albert II., 1967
S.K.H. Olav V., König von Norwegen, 1968
S. Excl. Manlio Brosio, NATO Generalsekretär, 1970
S. Excl. Varahagiri Venkata Giri, Staatspräsident der Republik Indien, 1970
S.D. Fürst Franz Josef II. und Gina von Liechtenstein, 1970
Robert McNamara, Präsident der Weltbank, 1970
S.Excl. Sithu U Thant, Uno Generalsekretär, 1971
S.Excl. Tun Abdul Razak, Premierminister von Malaysia, 1972
S.Excl. Giovanni Leone, Staatspräsident der Republik Italien, 1973
Général François Maurin, Chef d'état major des forces françaises, 1975
S. Excl. Mariano Rumor, Aussenminister der Republik Italien, 1975
S.K.H. Hassan ibn Talal, Kronprinz von Jordanien, 1975
Hildegard Knef, deutsche Schauspielerin, 1976
S. Excl. Gaston Thorn, Premierminister des Grossherzogtum Luxemburg, 1976
S. Excl. Mobutu Sese Seko, Staatspräsident der demokratischen Republik Kongo, 1976
Annelise Rothenberger, Opernsängerin, 1976
S. Excl. İhsan Sabri Çağlayangil, Türkischer Aussenminister, 1977
S. Excl. Otto Rösch, Verteidigungsminister der Republik Österreich, 1977
Sophia Loren, italienische Schauspielerin, 1978
Max von Sydow, schwedischer Schauspieler, 1978
John Cassavetes, US-amerikanischer Schauspieler und Regisseur, 1978
S.Excl. Kurt Waldheim, UNO-Generalsekretär, 1978
S. Excl. Moshe Dayan, Aussenminister von Israel, 1978
S. Excl. Dr. Hans-Jochen Vogel, Justizminister der Bundesrepublik Deutschland, 1979
S.K.H. Juan Carlos I. und Sofia, König und Königin von Spanien, 1979
José Carreras, spanischer Tenor, 1979
S.K.H. Prinz Philip, Duke of Edinburgh, 1979
S.Excl. Peter Veress, Aussenminister der Republik Ungarn, 1980
S.Excl. Boutros Boutros-Ghali, ägyptischer Ministerpräsident und späterer UNO Generalsekretär, 1980

S.K.H. Elizabeth II., Königin von England, 1980
S.Excl. Juvénal Habyarimana, Staatspräsident von Ruanda, 1980
S. Excl. Robert D. Muldoon, Premierminister von Neuseeland, 1980
S.K.H. Prinz Sultan ibn Abdulaziz ibn Saoud, Verteidigungsminister des Königreichs Saudi-Arabien, 1980
S.Excl. Jean François-Poncet, Aussenminister der französischen Republik, 1980
S. Excl. Emilio Colombo, Aussenminister der Republik Italien, 1981
S. Excl. Sandro Petrini, Staatspräsident der Republik Italien, 1981
S. Excl. Rudolf Kirchschläger, Bundespräsident der Republik Österreich, 1981
Shirley Bassey, britische Sängerin, 1981
Sir Alec Guinness, britischer Schauspieler, 1981
Emil Steinberger, Schweizer Kabarettist, 1981
Placido Domingo, spanischer Opernsänger, 1982
Georges Moustaki, französischer Komponist, 1982
Karel Gott, tschechischer Sänger, 1982
S. Excl. Gaston Thorn, Präsident der Europäischen Kommission, 1982
S. Excl. Karl Carstens, Präsident der Bundesrepublik Deutschland, 1982
Johannes Simmel, österreichischer Schriftsteller, 1983
Hazy Osterwald, Schweizer Musiker und Bandleader, 1983
Jupp Derwall, deutscher Bundestrainer, 1983
Roberto Blanco, deutscher Sänger, 1984
Edward Asner, US-amerikanischer Schauspieler und Filmproduzent, 1984
Mary Steenburgen, US-amerikanische Schauspielerin, 1984
S.K.H. Prinz Philip, Duke of Edinburgh, 1984
S.K.H. Carl XVI. Gustav und Silvia, König und Königin von Schweden, 1985
Ivan Rebroff, deutscher Sänger, 1985
Supertramp, britische Pop- und Rockband, 1986
S. Excl. Mauno Koivisto, Staatspräsident der Republik Finnland, 1986
Angelo Branduardi, italienischer Musiker und Songschreiber, 1986
Prince, US-amerikanischer Sänger, 1987
S. Excl. Chaim Herzog, Staatspräsident von Israel, 1987
S. Excl. Richard von Weizsäcker, Präsident der Bundesrepublik Deutschland, 1987
S. Excl. Franz Vranitzky, Bundeskanzler der Republik Österreich, 1988
S. Excl. Frank Charles Carlucci III., Verteidigungsminister der USA, 1988

S. Excl. Javier Pérez de Cuéllar, UNO-Generalsekretär, 1988
S. Excl. Mário Soares, Staatspräsident der Republik Portugal, 1988
S. Excl. Felipe González, Ministerpräsident des Königreichs Spanien, 1988
S. Excl. Giulio Andreotti, Ministerpräsident der Republik Italien, 1988
S. Excl. Helmut Kohl, Bundeskanzler der Bundesrepublik Deutschland, 1989
S. Excl. Hans Dietrich Genscher, Aussenminister der Bundesrepublik Deutschland, 1989
S. Excl. Boutros Boutros-Ghali, UNO-Generalsekretär, 1992
Michail Gorbatschow, ehem. Präsident der Sowjetunion, 1993
S.K.H. Beatrix, Königin der Niederlande und Prinz Claus, 1993
Alberto Lysy, argentinischer Violinist und Dirigent, 1994
Sir Yehudi Menuhin, Violinist und Dirigent, 1994
Claude Nicolier, Schweizer ESA Astronaut, 1994
Senta Berger, deutsche Schauspielerin, 1994
S. Excl. Eduardo Frei Ruiz-Tagle, Staatspräsident der Republik Chile, 1995
The Doobie Brothers, US-amerikanische Rockband, 1995
S. Excl. Aníbal Cavaco Silva, Premierminister der Republik Portugal, 1995
S. Excl. Desmond Tutu, Südafrikanischer Erzbischof und Friedensnobelpreisträger, 1995
S. Excl. Roman Herzog, Präsident der Bundesrepublik Deutschland, 1995
Juliette Greco, französische Chansonsängerin, 1996
S. Excl. Leonid Kutschma, Staatspräsident der Republik Ungarn, 1996
Bonnie Tylor, walisische Rocksängerin, 1996
S. Excl. Jean-Bertrand Aristide, Staatspräsident der Republik Haiti, 1996
S. Excl. Michael Ferris, Parlamentspräsident der Republik Irland, 1996
S. Excl. Liu Huaqing, Mitglied des Politbüros der Volksrepublik China, 1996
S. Excl. Oscar Luigi Scalfaro, Staatspräsident der Republik Italien, 1996
S. Excl. Mario Soares, Staatspräsident der Republik Portugal, 1996
Johannes Mario Simmel, österreichischer Schriftsteller, 1996
S. Excl. Hennadiy Udovenko, Aussenminister der Ukraine, 1997
S. Excl. Mendsaikhani Enkhsaikhan, Ministerpräsident der Mongolei, 1997
S. Excl. Wiktor Stepanowitsch Tschernomyrdin, Ministerpräsident der Russischen Föderation, 1997
S.K.H. Kronprinz Hassan bin Talal und Prinzessin Sarwath von Jordanien, 1997
Maximilian Schell, deutscher-schweizer Schauspieler, 1997
Johnny Cash, US-amerikanischer Musiker, 1997
S.K.H. Hussein I. und Noor, König und Königin von Jordanien, 1997
S. Excl. Nelson Mandela, Staatspräsident der Republik Südafrika, 1997
S. Excl. Kofi Annan, UNO-Generalsekretär, 1997
S. Excl. Martti Ahtisaari, Staatspräsident der Republik Finnland, 1997
S. Excl. Li Lanquing, Vize Premierminister der Volksrepublik China, 1998
Patricia Kaas, französische Sängerin, 1998
S. Excl. Fidel Castro Ruz, Staatspräsident von Kuba, 1998
Emil Steinberger, Schweizer Kabarettist, 1998
S. Excl. Jewgeni M. Primakow, Aussenminister der Russischen Föderation, 1998
Herbert Grönemeyer, deutscher Musiker, 1998
S. Excl. Aleksander Kwaśniewski, Staatspräsident der Republik Polen, 1998
Horst Tappert, deutscher Schauspieler, 1998
S. Excl. Jacques Chirac, Staatspräsident der Französischen Republik, 1998
Miriam Makeba, südafrikanische Sängerin, 1998
Mika Häkkinen, finnischer Formel 1 Weltmeister, 1998
S. Excl. Árpád Göncz, Staatspräsident der Republik Ungarn, 1999
S. Excl. Jiang Zemin, Staatspräsident der Volksrepublik China, 1999
S. Excl. Rudolf Scharping, Verteidigungsminsiter der Bundesrepublik Deutschland, 1999
S. Excl. Jorge Sampaio, Staatspräsident der Republik Portugal, 1999
S. Excl. Eduardo Serra Rexach, Verteidigungsminister des Königreichs Spanien, 1999
Michail Sergejewitsch Gorbatschow, russischer Friedensnobelpreisträger, 1999
Sophia Loren, italienische Filmschauspielerin, 2000
S. Excl. David Lévy, Aussenminister von Israel, 2000
S. Excl. Johannes Rau, Präsident der Bundesrepublik Deutschland, 2000
S.K.H. Prince Charles, Fürst von Wales und Herzog von Cornwall, 2000
S.K.H. Albert II und Paola, König und Königin von Belgien, 2000
Montserrat Caballé, spanische Opernsängerin, 2000
John le Carré, englischer Schriftsteller, 2001
S.Excl. Václav Havel, Staatspräsident der Tschechischen Republik, 2001
Laura Pausini, italienische Popsängerin, 2001
S. Excl. Carlo Azeglio Ciampi, Staatspräsident von Italien, 2003
Arthur Cohn, Schweizer Filmproduzent und Oscar-Preisträger, 2003
Thabo Mvuyelwa Mbeki, Präsident der Republik Südafrika, 2003
Kofi Atta Annan, UNO-Generalsekretär, 2003
Alanis Morissette, kanadische- US-amerikanische Sängerin, 2003
S.Excl. Igor Iwanow, Aussenminister der Russischen Föderation, 2003
S.Excl. Ion Iliescu, Staatspräsident von Rumänien, 2003
S.Excl. Mohammad Khatami, Staatspräsident des Iran, 2004
S.K.H. Prinz Saud Al-Faisal Al Saud, Aussenminsiter des Königreich Saudi Arabien, 2004
S.Excl. Vicente Fox, Staatspräsident von Mexiko, 2004
Bischof Amédée Grab, aus Anlass des Besuchs von Papst Johannes Paul II, 2004
Claudia Schiffer, deutsches Model, 2005
S. Excl. A. P. J. Abdul Kalam, Staatspräsident der Republik Indien, 2005
S.Excl. Georgi Parwanow, Staatspräsident von Bulgarien, 2006
S.K.H. Harald und Sonja, König und Königin von Norwegen, 2006
S. Excl. Fouad Siniora, Premierminister des Libanon, 2006
S. Excl. Heinz Fischer, Bundespräsident der Republik Österreich, 2006
S. Excl. Valdas Adamkus, Präsident der Republik Litauen, 2006
S. Excl. Michelle Bachelet, Präsidentin der Republik Chile, 2007
Herbert Grönemeyer, deutscher Sänger, 2007
Alinghi-Team, 2007
Karl-Heinz Böhm, österreichischer Schauspieler, 2007
S. Excl. Traian Basescu, Präsident von Rumänien, 2007
Stephan Eicher, Schweizer Chansonnier, 2007
Emil Steinegger, Schweizer Kabarettist, 2008
S. Excl. Ban Ki-Moon, UNO-Generalsekretär, 2008
S. Excl. José Manuel Barroso, Präsident der Europäischen Kommission, 2008
S. Excl. Jozefina Topalli, Präsidentin des albanischen Parlaments, 2008

S. Excl. László Sólyom, Staatspräsident von Ungarn, 2008
S. Excl. Wen Jiabao, Ministerpräsident der Volksrepublik China, 2009
Tracey Emin, britische Künstlerin, 2009
Dirk Bach, deutscher Schauspieler und Komiker, 2009
S. Excl. Wiktor Juschtschenko, Präsident der Republik Ukraine, 2009
Bruce Springsteen, US-amerikanischer Rockmusiker, 2009
Dexter Holland, Sänger Punkband the Offspring, 2009
S. Excl. Dmitri Medvedev, Ministerpräsident der Russischen Föderation, 2009
S. Excl. Ilham Aliyev, Präsident von Aserbaidschan, 2009
Paulo Coelho, brasilianischer Schriftsteller, 2009
Bruno Ganz, Schweizer Schauspieler, 2010
Thomas Hürlimann, Schweizer Schriftsteller, 2010
Sir Bob Geldof, irischer Rockmusiker, 2010
Holländische Nationalmannschaft, EM in Bern, 2010
S. Excl. Minh Triet Ngguyen, Präsident der Sozialistischen Republik Vietnam, 2010
S. Excl. Djibril Cavaye Yeguie, Parlamentspräsident von Kamerun, 2010
Muse, britische Rockband, 2010
Admiral James Stavridis, Supreme Allied Commander, Europe, 2010
Didier Drogba, ivorischer Fussballspieler, 2010
Lang Lang, chinesischer Pianist, 2010
S.Excl. John Atta Mills, Präsident der Republik Ghana, 2010
S. Excl. Christian Wulff, Präsident der Bundesrepublik Deutschland, 2010
Peter Gabriel, englischer Musiker und Videokünstler, 2010
S.K.H. Carl XVI. Gustaf, König von Schweden, 2010
Toni Blair, ehem. Premierminister des Vereinigten Königreichs, 2010
S. Excl. Jigme Thinley, Ministerpräsident des Königreich Bhutan, 2010
S. Excl. Abdullah Gül, Staatspräsident der Republik Türkei, 2010
Nek, italienischer Popsänger, 2010
S. Excl. Franco Frattini, Aussenminister von Italien, 2011
S. Excl. Serzh Azati Sargsyan, Präsident der Republik Armenien, 2011
S. Excl. Charles Aznavour, Chansonnier und armenischer Botschafter in der Schweiz, 2011
S.K.H. Juan Carlos und Sofia, König und Königin von Spanien, 2011
S. Excl. Lytvyn Volodymyr, Parlamentspräsident der Ukraine, 2011
Roger Federer, Schweizer Tennisspieler, 2011
Jamiroquai, britische Acid-Jazz Band, 2011
S. Excl. Pratibha Patil, Staatspräsidentin der Republik Indien, 2011
S. Excl. Theo-Ben Gurirab, Präsident der Interparlamentarischen Union, 2011
S. Excl. Meira Kumar, Parlamentspräsidentin der Republik Indien 2011
Carl Lewis, US-amerikanischer Leichtathlet, 2012
S. Excl. Aung San Suu Kyi, Politikerin und Parlamentsmitglied der Union Myanmar, 2012
Norah Jones, US-amerikanische Sängerin, 2012
Lenny Kravitz, US-amerikanischer Rocksänger, 2012
italienische Fussball-Nationalmannschaft, 2012
S. Excl. Ivan Gašparovič, Staatspräsident Slowakischen Republik, 2012
S. Excl. Bronislaw Komorowksi, Staatspräsident der Republik Polen, 2012
S. Excl. Mahmoud Abbas, Präsident der Palästinensischen Autonomiebehörde, 2012
S. Excl. Erato Kozakou-Marcoullis, Aussenministerin der Republik Zypern, 2012
S. Excl. Hui Liangyu, Vize-Premierminister der Volksrepublik China, 2013
Bille August, dänischer Filmregisseur, 2013
Jeremy Irons, britischer Schauspieler, 2013
Peter Bieri, alias Pascal Mercier, Schweizer Schriftsteller, 2013
Christopher Lee, britischer Schauspieler, 2013

165 Abreise des peruanischen Staatspräsidenten Manuel Prado y Ugarteche, 1960. – Departure of the President of Peru, Manuel Prado y Ugarteche, 1960.

Anmerkungen
Notes

1 Zur Definition von «Gasthof» und «Hotel»: Nikolaus Pevsner. A History of Building Types. (Princeton N.J. 1976. Deutsche Ausgabe: Funktion und Form. Die Geschichte der Bauwerke des Westens, mit einem Nachwort von Karen Michels, Hamburg 1998).
2 Stefan von Bergen. Jürg Steiner. Wie viel Bern braucht die Schweiz? Bern 2012.
3 Rudolf Gallati, Christoph Wyss. Unspunnen. Die Geschichte der Alphirtenfeste. Unterseen 1993.
4 Monica Bilfinger. Der Bernerhof in Bern. Schweizerische Kunstführer GSK, Nr. 770, Bern 2005, S. 18f.
5 25 Jahre Bellevue Palace Grand Hotel & Bernerhof Bern. Festschrift 1938.
6 Othmar Birkner. Bauen + Wohnen in der Schweiz 1850–1920, Basel 1975, S. 131.
7 Jura Brüschweiler in: Zeitschrift «du» 1998, Heft Nr. 8, S. 51.
8 Hugh Wilson. Lehrjahre eines Diplomaten. Deutsche Verlagsanstalt Stuttgart 1938.
9 Rainer Maria Rilke und die Schweiz: eine Ausstellung der Präsidialabteilung der Stadt Zürich, Strauhof Zürich, 25. September 1992 bis 10. Januar 1993. Katalog von Nicolas Baerlocher und Martin Bircher; wiss. Leitung und hrsg. von Jacob Steiner. Zürich [1992].
10 Die Schweizerische Nationalbank in Bern. Eine illustrierte Chronik (Pages blanches, Band 1), Bern 2011. S. 78.
11 Ebenda.

1 On the distinction between inn and hotel, see Nikolaus Pevsner. A History of Building Types. Princeton N.J. / London 1976, p. 169ff.
2 Stefan von Bergen. Jürg Steiner. Wie viel Bern braucht die Schweiz? Bern 2012 (How much Berne does Switzerland need?).
3 Rudolf Gallati, Christoph Wyss. Unspunnen. Die Geschichte der Alphirtenfeste. Unterseen 1993 (a history of the alpine festivals at Unspunnen).
4 Monica Bilfinger. Der Bernerhof in Bern. Schweizerische Kunstführer GSK, no. 770, Bern 2005, p. 18f (Guides to Swiss Monuments, essay on the Bernerhof hotel).
5 25 Jahre Bellevue Palace Grand Hotel & Bernerhof Bern. Festschrift 1938 (25th anniversary publication).
6 Othmar Birkner. Bauen + Wohnen in der Schweiz 1850–1920, Basle 1975, p. 131. (Construction and Housing in Switzerland).
7 Jura Brühschweiler: du 1998, no. 8, p. 51 (*du*, cultural magazine).
8 Hugh Wilson. Diplomat between Wars. New York: Longmans, Green, 1941.
9 Rainer Maria Rilke und die Schweiz: eine Ausstellung der Präsidialabteilung der Stadt Zürich, Strauhof Zürich, 25 September 1992–10 January 1993. Catalogue by Nicolas Baerlocher and Martin Bircher; Jacob Steiner, scientific editor. Zürich [1992] (Exhibition catalogue, Rilke and Switzerland).
10 R.M. Rilke. Poems, 1906 to 1926. Translated by J.B. Leishman. Hogarth Press, 1957.
11 Translated by Margret Powell-Joss.
12 Die Schweizerische Nationalbank in Bern. Eine illustrierte Chronik (Pages blanches, vol. 1), Bern 2011. p. 78 (illustrated chronicles on the Swiss National Bank in Berne).
13 Ibid.

Quellen / Bibliografie
Credits / Bibliography

Bauakten und Personenverzeichnisse im Stadtarchiv Bern / Architectural files and personal records at Berne State Archives. Firmenarchiv des Hotels Bellevue Palace in der Burgerbibliothek Bern / Hotel company archives at Burgerbibliothek Berne. Max Hofmann. Palace-Hotel Bellevue in Bern. In: Schweizerische Bauzeitung, 1915, vol. 65, p. 11ff, Zurich 1915. – L. Greiner, Chief engineer. Die Heizungs- und Lüftungsanlagen im Palace-Hotel Bellevue in Bern. In: Schweizerische Bauzeitung, 1915, vol. 65, pp. 15ff, Zurich 1915 (on heating and ventilation, Bellevue Palace Hotel). – Terner und Chopard, Engineers, Zürich. Die Eisenbetonkonstruktionen des Palace-Hotels Bellevue in Bern. In: Schweizerische Bauzeitung, 1915, vol. 65, p. 26ff, 40ff, Zurich 1915 (on reinforced concrete structures, Bellevue Palace Hotel). – Othmar Birkner. Bauen und Wohnen in der Schweiz. 1850–1920. Zürich 1975 (architecture and interior design in Switzerland). – Rainer Maria Rilke und die Schweiz: eine Ausstellung der Präsidialabteilung der Stadt Zürich, Strauhof Zürich, 25. September 1992–10 January 1993. Catalogue by Nicolas Baerlocher and Martin Bircher; Jacob Steiner, scientific editor. Zürich [1992] (exhibition catalogue, Rilke and Switzerland). – Rudolf Gallati, Christoph Wyss. Unspunnen. Die Geschichte der Alphirtenfeste. Unterseen 1993 (a history of the alpine festivals at Unspunnen). – Nadine Olonetzky. Aus den Annalen des Bellevue Palace. In: du, no. 8, Zurich, August 1998, p. 72ff (from the annals of the Bellevue Palace Hotel). – Silvia Kappeler-Bracher and Martin Fröhlich. Hotel Bellevue Palace Bern. Dokumentierte Baugeschichte und Planungsempfehlungen. Polycopy. Berne, September 1999 (documents of construction history and planners' advice). – Monica Bilfinger and Martin Fröhlich. Hotel Bellevue Palace Bern. Inventar Möbel und Ausstattung 1913–1970. Polycopy. Berne, October 1999 (inventory, furniture and interior furnishings). – Monica Bilfinger and Martin Fröhlich. Hotel Bellevue Palace Bern. Inventar Kunstsammlung bis 1975. Polycopy. Berne, May 2001 (inventory, art collection). – Roland Flückiger-Seiler. Hotel Träume zwischen Gletschern und Palmen. Baden 2001 (on hotel architecture between glaciers and palm trees). – Belle-View. Informationsblätter im Jahr der Erneuerung, nos. 1–7. Berne 2002/03 (collection of information leaflets in year of refurbishment). – Roland Flückiger-Seiler. Hotel Paläste zwischen Traum und Wirklichkeit. Schweizer Tourismus und Hotelbau 1830–1920. Baden 2003 (on Swiss tourism and hotel architecture, 1830–1920). – Hans Rudolf Fuhrer, Paul Meinrad Strässle (eds.). General Ulrich Wille. Vorbild den einen – Feindbild den anderen. Zürich 2003 (on Gen. U. Wille). – Monica Bilfinger. Der Bernerhof in Bern. Schweizerische Kunstführer GSK, Nr. 770, Bern 2005. – Martin Fröhlich. Das Hotel Bellevue Palace in Bern. Schweizerische Kunstführer GSK, no. 798 (German/English), Berne 2006. – Peter Kamber. Geheime Agentin. Berlin 2010. – Anne-Marie Biland. Warenhäuser in der Stadt Bern. Ein Beitrag zur lokal gefärbten Warenhaus-Architektur kurz vor und nach 1900. Edited by bauforschungonline.ch, Berne 2011 (on Bernese department stores around 1900). – Stefan von Bergen, Jürg Steiner. Wie viel Bern braucht die Schweiz? Berne 2012 (How much Berne does Switzerland need?).

Bildnachweis
Photo Credits

Basel, Club Grand Hotel & Palace:
Basel, Club Grand Hotel & Palace: Abb. 59
Basel, Schule für Gestaltung Basel, Plakatsammlung: Abb. 1
Berlin, Hotel Adlon Kempinski: Abb. 45
Bern, Burgerbibliothek: Abb. 6, 7, 11, 13, 20, 24, 31, 32, 43, 51, 81, 82, 83
Bern, Burgerbibliothek, Firmenarchiv des Hotels Bellevue Palace Bern: Abb. 14, 17, 18, 19, 21, 22, 25, 26, 27, 42, 46, 47, 48, 53, 63, 66, 67, 68, 69, 70, 71, 72, 73, 74, 77, 78, 79, 80, 85, 86, 88, 89, 90, 91, 92, 93, 94, 95, 96, 97, 98, 99, 100, 101, 102, 103, 104, 105, 106, 107, 108, 109, 112, 113, 114, 115, 116, 117, 118, 119, 120, 121, 122, 123, 124, 127, 128, 131, 132, 133, 135, 136, 137, 140, 141, 142, 143, 145, 146, 149, 150, 151, 152, 153, 154, 155, 156, 158, 161, 162, 165
Bern, Hotel Bellevue Palace: Abb. 41, 44, 58, 75, 76, 87, 91, 110, 111, 129, 130, 134, 138, 139, 144, 147, 148, 157, 159, 160, 163, 164
Bern, Kunstmuseum: Abb. 9, 12
Bern, Schweizerische Nationalbibliothek, Graphische Sammlung: Abb. 3, 5
Bern, Schweizerische Nationalbibliothek, Schweizerisches Literaturarchiv: Abb. 54, 56, 57
Bern, Staatsarchiv: Abb. 49, 125, 126
London, National Gallery: Abb. 10
Privatbesitz: Abb. 2, 4, 55, 64, 65
Reproduktionen aus: Monica Bilfinger. Der Bernerhof in Bern. Schweizerische Kunstführer GSK, Nr. 770, Bern 2005, S. 20, 29: Abb. 15, 23 – «du» Die Zeitschrift der Kultur 1998, Heft 3, S. 58: Abb. 62; 1998, Heft 8, S. 51: Abb. 52 – Martin Fröhlich. Das Hotel Bellevue Palace in Bern, 2006 (siehe Bibliografie), S. 36: Abb. 84 – H. R. Furrer, P. M. Strässle. General Ulrich Wille 2003 (siehe Bibliografie), Taf. XIII: 50 – Internet: Abb. 28, 61 – Journal de Genève, Ausgabe vom 5. März 1865: Abb. 16. – Schweizerische Bauzeitung 1913, Bd. 62, Heft 3: Abb. 8; 1915, Bd. 65, Hefte 2, 3, 4: Abb. 29, 30, 33, 34, 35, 36, 37, 38; 1960, Bd. 78, Heft 48: Abb. 40; 1965, Bd. 83, Heft 10: Abb. 39;

Achevé d'imprimer sur les presses de l'imprimerie Gasser SA
Le Locle (CH)
2013

Imprimé en Suisse